CROCHETTERIE

D1492118

Quarto is the authority on a wide range of topics.

Quarto educates, entertains and enriches the lives of
our readers – enthusiasts and lovers of hands-on living.

www.QuartoKnows.com

First published in the English language in 2016 by

Jacqui Small LLP
74–77 White Lion Street
London N1 9PF

www.jacquismallpub.com

Photography: Konsta Linkola
Graphic design: Oona Viskari
English translation: Mirette El Rafie

ISBN: 978 1 91025 489 9

A catalogue record for this book is available from
the British Library.

10 9 8 7 6 5 4 3 2 1

Printed in China

Molla Mills

CROCHETTERIE

Cool Contemporary Crochet for the Creatively Minded

jacqui
small

HANDICRAFTS AUTHOR, MOLLA MILLS, is a southern Ostrobothnian crochet-guru whose books are published all over the world. *Crochetterie* took 14 months of work and 28 kilos of yarn. Much of the yarn was crocheted and unravelled, rolled into balls, and crocheted again: part of it has ended up in the test-piece drawer as a reminder of how a good handicrafts project is born.

INTRODUCTION

Crochetterie is the next in a series of crochet instruction books, the first of which began life five years ago during my studies at the School of Arts and Design. That initial project has since grown to enormous proportions, with books currently available in seven different languages. This hobby of mine has developed into a career I am passionate about, and I can now happily declare myself to be a professional crocheter. I was supposed to become something else, but if you can do something well, you want to show it to the whole world, and in those cases it doesn't pay to stand in the way of your own passion. I decided to turn my back on common sense and just go for it.

When I told my friends I wanted to create a crochet instruction guide that would appeal to men, their first reaction was astonished scepticism. They questioned whether men could really be enthusiastic about crochet. Why not, I thought. Technically speaking, crochet is downright engineer-level precise, and requires careful consideration with regards to sourcing materials, calculating wear resistance and colour choice. In Finland, crochet has long been a popular hobby among boys, with many a hat rack displaying their hand-crocheted beanies. I have also had male participants in my crochet seminars; although percentage-wise they are very few, this certainly doesn't curb their enthusiasm.

Crochet is suitable for everyone, and partaking is a great way to improve mood. However, it is important to master the technique from the outset. You will undoubtedly need to unravel work and start again, but remember that each remake will prove more successful. Practice requires patience, which is something even the professionals can struggle with. So be prepared, the ongoing journey will probably present you with more headaches than simply worrying about whether your stitches are too loose.

Work on the book began in the early winter of 2014, with an optimistic anticipation of new territorial conquests. First off, I got myself a good notebook; an A5 one with hard covers containing 128 pages of recycled paper. Over-preparedness at its finest. The notebook began to fill with ideas and colour-charts, and pages were scribbled with contact details, tips from friends and wow-moments, such as the time I spotted an attractive man wearing a fabulous jumper at the supermarket checkout. Ideas will quickly escape, so need to be captured in the moment. My old Nokia had not yet been upgraded to a more intelligent model, and in any case, my ideas seemed to take shape by being described by hand.

In mid-June I spent the final stretch of a six-hour bus journey to my holiday destination at an Eastern-European beach town completing the black and white Folk Bag. The bag turned out great, and I rejoiced, in a quietly Finnish way, because one of the makes for the book had succeeded, plus, I would soon arrive at the shores of the Black Sea and was looking forward to five weeks of sunbathing, collecting ideas in my notebook and partaking in some light crochet. By the end of the bus journey, however, my mood was completely different. My notebook of ideas and sketches had vanished! Someone had mistaken my chequered, MM-monogrammed laptop bag for their own, and so my beloved notebook had disappeared together with my laptop. I felt a complete loss of hope. All of my ideas had been lost, the complete contents of the book!

I drifted down the sun-baked boulevard in heavy spirits, wondering whether I should simply forget about the whole project. My local friends, of course, tried to be helpful, and encouraged me to buy a new laptop. What they didn't understand was that the most valuable thing in that bag had actually been my notebook. The only good thing about the laptop had been the Bang & Olufsen-built speaker system; the computer itself burned red hot in my lap.

I dropped into the local art supplies shop and picked at papers and felt-tip pens. I tried to smile politely at the handsome sales clerk, but only managed a tear-smudged grimace. How could I get my ideas back? Where would I even begin? The thought of someone tossing my notebook into the bin, as if it was worthless, sent shivers from the clasp of my bikini-top to the top of my scalp. I felt like screaming. I collected myself and, passing through the till, stepped outside with three black felt-tips and an A5-sized notebook with black covers and thick white pages.

I walked to the beach and picked out what looked like the best table in a fancy restaurant. A large tanker was moored on the horizon, the kind that sail the Black Sea carrying merchandise from one country to the next. This one's bow was pointing towards the Bosporus. My thoughts drifted across the sea to the colourful bazaars and handicrafts quarters of Istanbul, where men and women sit weaving carpets and embroidering textiles. I remembered one particular trip to Tryavna in Bulgaria, and recalled the local village crafters tanning leather or sculpting woodcuts in their workshops; they were all men. I thought of the other handcrafters in the village, weaving, sewing, building and whittling. Again, they were men. Recalling then my own father, who taught me woodworking and who built my mother a loom, I made the decision to not give up on my project, but to finish the book, no matter what.

I scribbled a hundred new ideas in the first pages of my new notebook, and on the inside cover added the text 'If you find this, please return it to me', accompanied by my email address. On my return to Finland, the covers of the notebook were hanging off and the pages contained another 185 new ideas.

The months after my return were spent crocheting in my workroom. Crochet instructions are definitely not born on the first try, and the idea is only refined through practice: you wouldn't believe how many test pieces can be found in my drawers. The neck warmer (page 88) was originally a woolly hat, the football bag (page 196) was a fisherman's trap, and I crocheted the wayfarer's jumper (page 74) twice from beginning to end. The first time the jumper was so large over the shoulders you would have needed to wear American football gear underneath. In the end, it became so nicely fitted that I used the same instructions for my own red top, and for my little niece's summer dress. One good set of instructions turned into many!

In the photo on the previous spread, I am concentrating on sewing an anchor bag that never made it into the book. Instead, I made a new and better design, replacing the grey anchor with a red one – a symbol visible from a long way off. The bag's anchor motif is a reminder of the troubles that can plague any project. It prompts me to remember the importance of my own work, which can sometimes be forgotten in all the hustle and bustle. I exchanged my day job for the insecurity of being a professional handicrafts author, and I'm still following that same path. The journey may be full of storms, but the horizon always opens up ahead.

In regards to the storage of ideas and drafts, I still use the notebook and write everything down by hand. I do, however, take photos of the pages and store them in the memory of my new, intelligent phone.

Molla

ABBREVIATIONS AND DIFFICULTY LEVELS

Memorizing crochet abbreviations (detailed below) will help you to read and follow the instructions as you crochet. Crochet terminology differs between the UK and the US; in this book, US terms are given in parentheses.

Each project in this book has a difficulty level, to help you decide whether a make suits your current ability, as well as further information regarding time or extra equipment required, where relevant.

The works crocheted using two- and three-colour techniques, as well as pixel crochets, are accompanied by crochet charts. A chart features a symbol for each stitch, so reading one takes a bit of practice. Text directions for the first few rows or rounds of the crochet are also included, however, to help you get started with reading the charts.

 Effortless crochet work, suitable for the beginner and the speed-crocheter

 Tricky crochet work, but can be managed, even with little patience

 Demanding crochet work, requires previous experience, or help from a practised crocheter

 Time-consuming crochet work, worth reserving a few evenings, or even a couple of months, for

 Sewing bits, this crochet work requires sewing by hand or with a sewing machine

ch chain stitch

dc (sc) double crochet (single crochet)

ss slip stitch

st stitch

rnd round

tr (dc) treble crochet (double crochet) or pillar

yoh yarn over hook

TOOLS

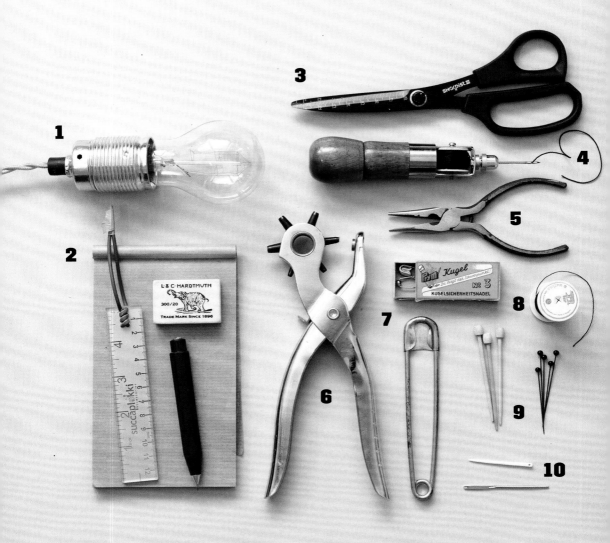

1. An extra lamp for twilight handicrafts
2. Note-taking tools, ruler
3. Sharp scissors
4. Sewing awl for working with leather
5. Pliers might be required to help the needle when finishing with thick yarn
6. Hole punch
7. Safety pins
8. Strong sewing thread
9. Bamboo and metal dressmakers' pins
10. Bone needle and tapestry needle

CROCHET HOOKS

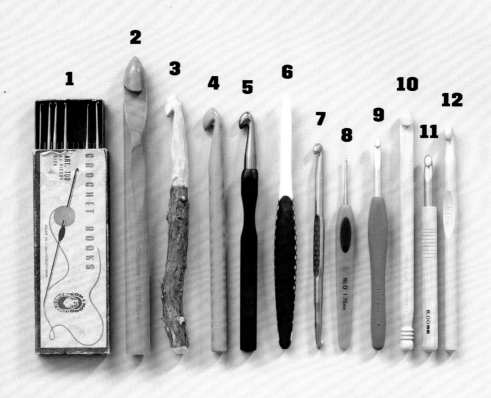

1 Thin, Czech, metal hooks from the 1950s

2 Wooden thick hook, 15.75 mm (Q)

3 Own-made hook, whittling instructions page 258

4 Recycled-plastic thick hook, 10.0 mm (N/15)

5 American angular hook, 8.0 mm (L/11)

6 Prym's ergonomic hook, 7.0 mm (K/10.5)

7 Two-headed metal hook, 5.0 mm (H/8) and 6.0 mm (J/10)

8 Thin ergonomic hook in a plastic holder

9 Ergonomic hook, 9.0 mm (M/13)

10 ChioaoGoon bamboo hook, 9.0 mm (M/13)

11 Kinki Amibar's metal-tipped bamboo hook, 6.0 mm (J/10)

12 Metal hook for rig crochet, 8.0 mm (L/11)

HOME

1

CARRY CUSHION

SIZE	YARN	HOOK
w: 50 cm (19¾ in) h: 25 cm (10 in)	Schachenmayr, Merino Extrafine, off-white three balls, dark green two balls. Weight of ball is 50 g (1¾ oz)	2.5 mm (B/1)

OTHER

Zip (zipper) l: 30 cm (12 in), two rivets, cushion insert 25 x 50 cm (10 x 19¾ in), leather strap l: 40 cm (15¾ in)

Back problems are the scourge of modern-day society, and a contributing factor may well be the mind-boggling number of hours we spend sitting each day. Therefore, it is important to consider good ergonomics at your workstation, whether at home or in an office or studio environment. Start by crocheting this cushion to support your lower back, and add a handle to make it easy to take with you to any workplace.

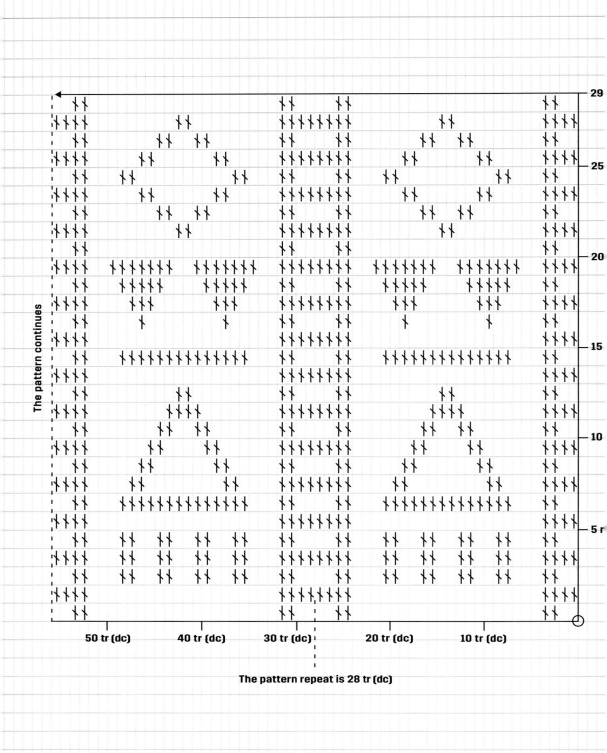

The pattern continues

50 tr (dc)   40 tr (dc)   30 tr (dc)   20 tr (dc)   10 tr (dc)

29

25

20

15

5 r

The pattern repeat is 28 tr (dc)

CROCHET INSTRUCTIONS

The make is crocheted using a two-colour pillar technique worked in a tube (see page 246 for step-by-step instructions). While crocheting, the non-working yarn is carried along within the pillars.

Rnd 1. Chain 224 stitches with the off-white yarn to begin, chaining loose stitches so they won't strain in the final make. Check that your work isn't twisted, then close it into a ring with a slip stitch. Ch 3 stitches with the off-white yarn to form the first pillar of the round. Switch to the green yarn on the last yarn over hook of the second pillar. Work 1 treble (double) crochet stitch with the green yarn and change back to the off-white yarn at the second pillar. Crochet 19 tr (dc) with the off-white yarn then change to the green yarn on the last yoh of the next pillar. Continue crocheting the round, following the chart and working four pattern repeats in total. Close the round with a ss in the third chain stitch from the beginning, making the yoh with the green yarn.

Rnd 2. Ch 3 stitches with the green yarn. Carry the off-white yarn, crochet 2 tr (dc) and change to the off-white at the third pillar. Crochet 19 tr (dc) with the off-white yarn and change to the green yarn on the last yoh of the next pillar. Continue working the round, following the chart. The round is always closed with a ss in the third chain stitch from the beginning.

Continue working, following the chart. There are a total of 29 rounds in the work. Cut the yarns and fasten off.

pillar, green

pillar, off-white

1   Pin the zip (zipper) in place in the middle of the cover's lower edge. Make sure the patterns align on both sides of the zip (zipper). Sew in place by hand or with a sewing machine, taking care not to stretch the edges of the crochet.

2   Sew closed the gaps at each end of the zip (zipper) by hand using off-white yarn, one stitch at a time.

3   The zip (zipper) will only show a little on the right side of the make. Make sure the crochet stitches don't get caught in the teeth of the zip (zipper).

4   Sew the upper edge closed by hand, one stitch at a time.

5   Measure a space for the leather strap in the middle of the cover's upper edge. Fold 3 cm (1¼ in) over on both ends of the strap. Punch holes through the strap and use rivets to close the overlap, then sew the handle to the crochet with strong sewing thread.

6   Once the cushion insert is inside the cover, the carry cushion is complete. To make a washable cushion cover, choose a cotton band for the handle.

5

6

STORAGE BASKET

SIZE	YARN	HOOK
d: 20 cm (8 in) h: 22 cm (8¾ in)	Jute yarn, approx. 600 g (21 oz)	6.0 mm (J/10)

OTHER	
Three metal rings d: 20 cm (8 in), thin leather belt l: 50 cm (19¾ in)	

Every home needs a place to house miscellaneous items, from shirt buttons and batteries to birthday candles and balls of string. A crocheted storage basket makes a convenient cache for these homeless bits and bobs. Put on the lid, and the chaos is gone!

TIP!
Enlarge this design to make a laundry basket, and crochet it using old rug weft. Or make a small lidless basket for a herb pot out of thin hemp cord.

Begin crocheting the storage basket from the bottom. The lid is crocheted separately.

1 **Rnd 1.** Wrap yarn twice around a finger and crochet 10 double (single) crochet stitches into the loop. Crochet the yarn end together with a few stitches, and at the end of the round pull the yarn so there is no hole left in the bottom.
Rnd 2. Crochet 2 dc (sc) into each stitch. From now on always put the hook through both loops of the stitch in the row below.
Rnd 3. Crochet 2 dc (sc) into every other stitch and 1 dc (sc) into the intervening stitches. The round consists of 30 dc (sc) altogether.
Rnd 4. Crochet 2 dc (sc) into every third stitch and 1 dc (sc) into the intervening stitches.
Rnd 5. Crochet a dc(sc)-round without any increases.
Rnd 6. Crochet 2 dc (sc) into every fourth stitch and 1 dc (sc) into the intervening stitches.
Rnd 7. Crochet a dc(sc)-round without any increases.

Rnd 8. Crochet 2 dc (sc) into every fifth stitch and 1 dc (sc) into the intervening stitches.
Rnd 9. Incorporate the first metal ring into the work, crocheting the stitches by taking the yarn over hook from below the metal ring. Crochet a dc(sc)-round: while crocheting the metal ring you will need to stretch the work a little. Remove a round if the base is too large compared to the size of the metal ring. If the base is too small, add a round or two.

2 **Rnds 10–31.** Crochet dc(sc)-rounds.

3 **Rnd 32.** In this round, crochet the second metal ring along with the stitches.

4 Finish the upper edge with a round of slip stitches. Cut the yarn and fasten off.

5 Crochet a lid following the instructions for the base up to rnd 8.
Rnd 9. Incorporate the third metal ring and crochet a dc(sc)-round. Crochet 3 dc (sc)

5

6

7

8

9

10

around the ring, miss (skip) one stitch and continue crocheting 29 dc (sc). Crochet 3 dc (sc) around the ring, miss (skip) one stitch and continue crocheting to the end of the round.

6 Finish the edge with a ss-round. Cut the yarn and fasten off. Cut 15-cm (6-in) of leather belt from the non-buckle end for the hinge.

7 Punch holes through the leather and slip it through one of the holes in the lid.

8 With strong thread, sew through the holes in the leather to sew the hinge to the inside of the lid and outside of the basket.

9 Cut 18 cm (7 in) of leather belt, slip it through the other hole in the lid and sew it in place on the inside.

10 Sew the buckle end of the belt onto the body of the basket in line with the lid belt. Punch holes in the leather to fasten the buckle.

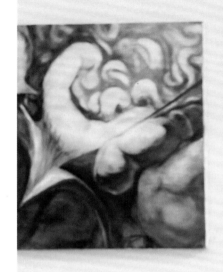

IN HIS WORKROOM IN Helsinki's Vallila district, French illustrator Paul is concentrating on creating new artwork. His exhibition in the Project Room gallery has just ended. Paul specializes in depicting the human body, and hands in particular; he also designs album covers. The storage basket is a perfect receptacle for art supplies, and the inevitable paint spatters bring the jute surface to life.

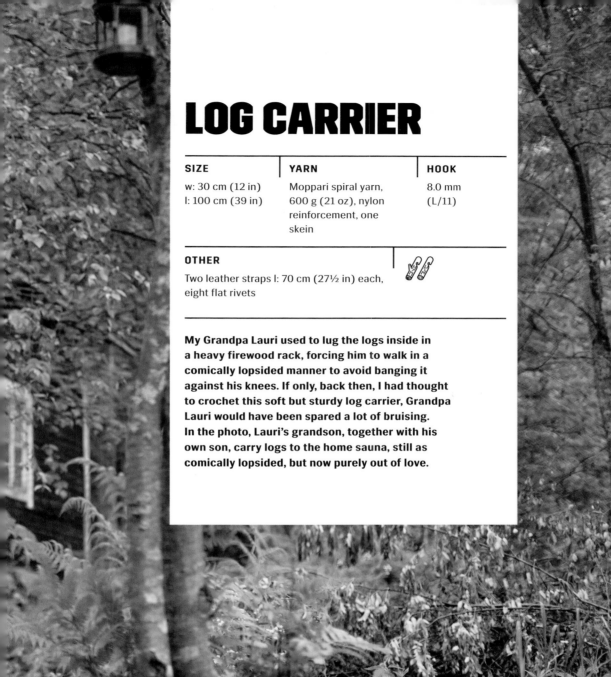

LOG CARRIER

SIZE	YARN	HOOK
w: 30 cm (12 in)	Moppari spiral yarn,	8.0 mm
l: 100 cm (39 in)	600 g (21 oz), nylon	(L/11)
	reinforcement, one	
	skein	

OTHER	
Two leather straps l: 70 cm (27½ in) each, eight flat rivets	

My Grandpa Lauri used to lug the logs inside in a heavy firewood rack, forcing him to walk in a comically lopsided manner to avoid banging it against his knees. If only, back then, I had thought to crochet this soft but sturdy log carrier, Grandpa Lauri would have been spared a lot of bruising. In the photo, Lauri's grandson, together with his own son, carry logs to the home sauna, still as comically lopsided, but now purely out of love.

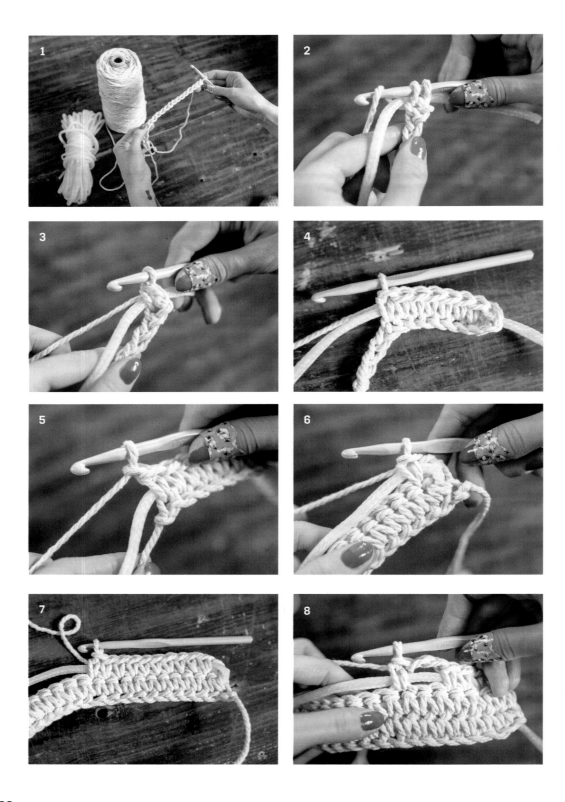

5 The row consists of 25 dc (sc). Carry the reinforcement along all the way to the last stitch. Ch 1 stitch to begin the second row.

6 **Row 2.** Carry the nylon reinforcement with you as you make the first stitch.

7 Crochet 1 dc (sc) into every stitch, putting the hook through both loops. Make sure the reinforcement isn't too loose or too taut within the stitches.

8 **Row 3.** This row will begin the holes for the handles. Ch 1 stitch at the beginning of the row. Carry the reinforcement along and crochet 6 dc (sc). Crochet 2 ch, miss (skip) two stitches then crochet 7 dc (sc). Crochet 2 ch, miss (skip) two stitches then crochet 7 dc (sc) to finish.

9 **Row 4.** Crochet 1 dc (sc) into each stitch. At the holes for the handle, crochet 2 dc (sc) into the ch-arch.

10 Crochet 60 dc(sc)-rows. Make holes for the handle at the other end of the log carrier, and finish both ends with ss-rows. Cut the yarn and fasten off.

11 The nylon reinforcement is carried neatly and evenly along the edges of the crochet. The reinforcement supports the make and increases its lifespan.

The make is worked back and forth while carrying the nylon reinforcement throughout.

1 **Row 1.** Chain 26 stitches to begin. Leave a yarn end of 150 cm (60 in): this will be used to crochet a row of slip stitch along the edge to finish it.

2 Put the hook through the second chain from the hook and catch the yarn over hook from below the nylon. Then put the hook over the nylon and catch another yoh.

3 Pull the yoh through to crochet a double (single) crochet stitch. The nylon reinforcement will stay inside the stitch.

4 Crochet a row of dc (sc) stitches in this way.

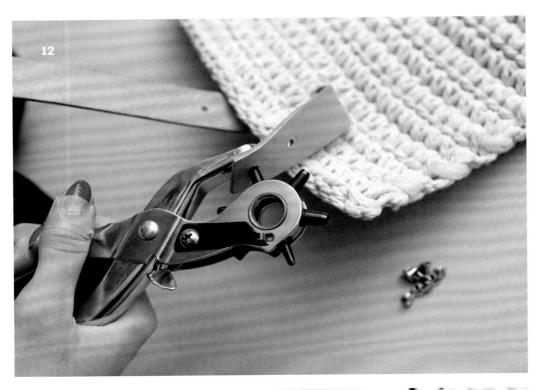

12 Cut some suitably long leather handles for
    your make, here they are 70 cm (27½ in)
    long. Make sure the handles are narrow
    enough to slip through the holes in the carrier
    without stretching them. Punch holes through
    the handles.

13 Fasten the handle loops with flat rivets, or sew
    them closed with strong yarn.

14 The log carrier is complete.

JETTY RUG

SIZE
w: 55 cm (21½ in)
l: 120 cm (47¼ in)

YARN
Esteri, off-white and red, 1 kg
(2 lb 3 oz) per colour, plastic tube
l: 20 m (21⅞ yd), d: 4 mm (¼ in)

HOOK
8.0 mm (L/11)

OTHER
Cotton strap l: 250 cm (98½ in)

The crochet for this project is a variation of that worked for the log carrier (see page 33). A 55-cm (21½-in) long plastic tube is crocheted into the beginning and end row of each stripe. In the middle of each stripe there are three rows of double (single) crochet without the tube.

Row 1. Chain 51 stitches with the off-white yarn to begin. Crochet a dc(sc)-row while carrying the plastic tube along throughout. The row consists of 50 stitches altogether.

Rows 2–4. Always ch 1 stitch at the start of each row. Crochet the dc(sc)-rows without the plastic tube.

Row 5. Crochet a dc(sc)-row while carrying the plastic tube along.

Row 6. Change to the red yarn and crochet a dc(sc)-row while carrying the plastic tube along.

Rows 7–9. Crochet the dc(sc)-rows without the plastic tube. Make sure there are always 50 dc (sc) in the row. Carry the plastic tube along the next row. Continue crocheting the colour stripes. Each stripe is always five rows high. Always cut the yarn and fasten it off within the stitches when the stripe colours change; that way there won't be any yarns hanging out at the edges of the rug. Crochet 19 stripes altogether. Cut the yarns and fasten off. At the end of the rug there is a 2.5-m (2¾-yd) long cotton carry handle, which is slipped through the stitches on the second row. The rug can be rolled up and the carry handle wrapped around it to tie it closed.

CHEQUERED RUG

SIZE	YARN	HOOK
w: 80 cm (31½ in) l: 240 cm (94½ in)	Muhku wool yarn, off-white 3 kg (6 lb 10 oz), grey 2 kg (4 lb 8oz)	7.0 mm (K/10.5)

This thick wool rug will keep your behind nice and toasty on the first, perhaps adventurous, picnic of the season as the weather begins to warm. Wool's best characteristic is its warmth, but another good trait is its ability to stay clean. The wool rug can simply be aired out after use.

TIP!
Crochet yourself a warm scarf for winter by using these same instructions. Simply use thinner wool.

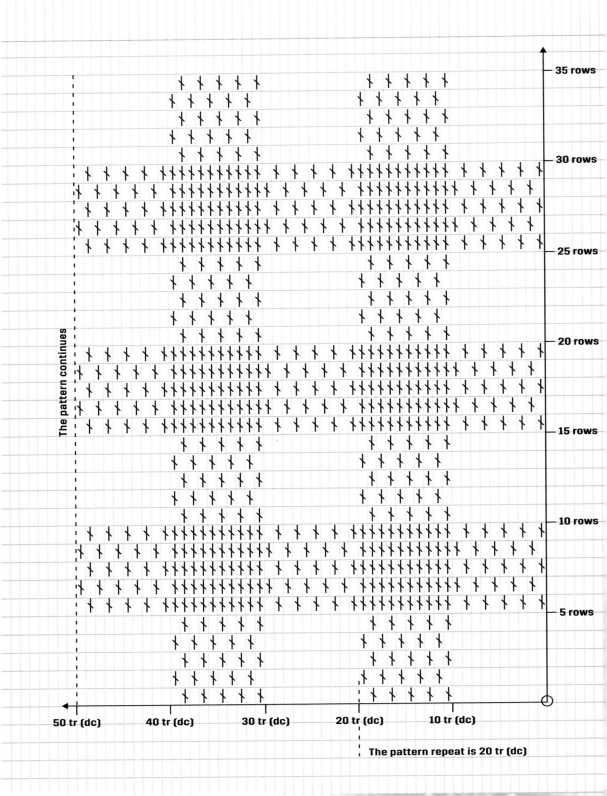

The pattern continues

50 tr (dc)　　40 tr (dc)　　30 tr (dc)　　20 tr (dc)　　10 tr (dc)

35 rows

30 rows

25 rows

20 rows

15 rows

10 rows

5 rows

The pattern repeat is 20 tr (dc)

CROCHET INSTRUCTIONS

The make is worked back and forth using a two-colour pillar technique (see page 248 for step-by-step instructions). Carry the non-working yarn along within the pillars throughout.

Row 1. Chain 72 stitches with the off-white yarn to begin. Leave a yarn end of 2 m (2⅛ yd): this will be used to crochet a row of double (single) crochet along the starting edge of the rug to finish it. Crochet the first pillar into the fourth chain stitch from the hook. Carry the grey yarn along and work 8 treble (double) crochet stitches with the off-white yarn. Change to the grey yarn on the last yarn over hook of the next pillar. Crochet the next pillar to the last yoh with the grey yarn, then change to the off-white yarn. Continue crocheting the following 9 tr (dc) by changing the yarn on the last yoh of each pillar. Continue working, following the chart and working the pattern repeat three times, then working the final 10-stitch block shown on the left of the chart. Crochet the last tr (dc) in the row without the grey yarn and finish by gently pulling on the grey yarn. The row consists of 70 tr (dc) altogether.

Row 2. Ch 3 stitches with the off-white yarn to form the first pillars in the row. Carry the grey yarn along. Crochet 8 tr (dc), putting the hook through both loops of the stitch in the row below. Crochet the ninth pillar to the last yoh with the off-white yarn before changing to the grey yarn. Continue crocheting the following 9 tr (dc) by changing the yarn on the last yoh of each pillar. Remember to pull on the yarn after each change of colour to avoid yarn loops. Leave the grey yarn one pillar from the end of the row.

Row 3. Always ch 3 stitches at the beginning of each row and carry the non-working yarn along from the first pillar. From now on the rows are crocheted by changing the grey and off-white yarn, following the chart. The colour always changes on the last yoh of the pillar. In each row the non-working yarn is carried along within the pillars, and only the first and last pillars are crocheted without a second yarn. This will ensure the yarn loops are not visible along the edge on the right side of the rug, but remain hidden on the reverse side.

When changing colours, always pull gently on the yarn carried along within the pillars, since a slack yarn will be visible on the right side of the make. Pulling the yarns ensures the rug has an even surface and straight edges.

Continue crocheting, following the chart. If the yarn runs out in the middle of the work, tie the ends together and continue crocheting. These yarns should be cut and fastened off within the pillars on the reverse side of the rug. Make sure that any knots also end up on the back of the rug.

The make consists of 115 rows altogether. Finish both short edges of the rug with a dc(sc)-row. Cut the yarn and fasten off.

pillar, grey

pillar, off-white

TOPI IS A SELF-TAUGHT CROCHETER and has made socks, gloves and jumpers for his daughter. He likes to use earthy wool yarns for his makes. Here he is completing a mitten using slip stitches worked in a tubular spiral. The result is a beautiful surface reminiscent of Tunisian crochet.

TIP!
Sew a large canvas bag by following the instructions for the anchor bag on page 144. The black and white geometric fabric in the photo is hand printed in Berlin. Daniel – whose start-up business, Colorblind Patterns, specializes in designing textile patterns – creates the fabrics.

PATTERN RUG

SIZE	YARN	HOOK
w: 80 cm (31½ in) l: 280 cm (110 in)	Lilli hollow yarn, beige 5 kg (11 lb), green 3.5 kg (7 lb 11 oz)	7.0 mm (K/10.5)

Two-year-old Aarni Olavi plays at home with his blocks on the edge of a long crocheted rug. The mint-green finish for the floor is inspired by colour fashions from the 1950s, and the large, soft rug conveniently covers the battered floor's scratches and protects from splinters. The room is so vast that it would take 35 rugs altogether to fill it. One is a good start though, as this rug's surface area is 2.24 m² (2⅜ yd²).

TIP!
Crochet a cool wall hanging using the same instructions. Instead of Lilli hollow yarn, use the Mini version, and fasten some tassels to the lower edge.

The pattern width is 60 tr (dc)

CROCHET INSTRUCTIONS

The make is crocheted back and forth using a two-colour pillar technique (see page 248 for step-by-step instructions). The non-working yarn is carried along within the pillars while working.

Row 1. Chain 62 stitches with the beige yarn to begin. Leave a yarn end of 2 m (2⅛ yd): this will be used to crochet a row of slip stitch along the starting edge of the rug to finish it. Crochet the first pillar into the fourth chain stitch from the hook. Carry the green yarn along and work 1 treble (double) crochet stitch into each chain stitch with the beige yarn. Crochet the last pillar of the row without the green yarn. Pull lightly on the green yarn at the end of the row to make sure it isn't left loose within the pillars. The row consists of 60 tr (dc) altogether.

Row 2. Ch 3 stitches with the beige yarn to form the first pillar of the row. Include the green yarn and carry it along to the penultimate pillar in the row. Continue crocheting 1 tr (dc) into each pillar, putting the hook through both loops of the stitch in the row below. At the end of the row, lightly pull on the carried yarn.

Row 3. In this row you will begin crocheting the pattern. Ch 3 stitches with the beige yarn. Carry the green yarn and crochet 2 tr (dc) with the beige yarn. On the last yarn over hook of the next pillar, change to the green yarn. Crochet 1 tr (dc) with the green yarn then change back to the beige yarn on the last yoh of the next pillar. The row consists of 3 tr (dc) with the beige yarn, 2 tr (dc) with the green yarn and 4 tr (dc) with

the beige yarn at the end of the row. Remember to gently pull on the yarn every time you change colours to avoid yarn loops.

Row 4. Always ch 3 stitches at the beginning of each row, and carry the non-working yarn along from the next pillar. The rows hereafter are crocheted by changing the beige and green yarns. The colour always changes on the last yoh of a pillar, with the non-working yarn carried within the pillars. Only the first and last pillar of each row is crocheted without the second yarn, which ensures that the yarn loops are not visible along the edge on the right side of the rug, but remain hidden on the reverse.

When changing colours, always pull gently on the yarn carried along within the pillars, since a slack yarn will be visible on the right side of the make. Pulling the yarns ensures the rug has an even surface and straight edges.

Continue crocheting, following the chart. If the yarn runs out in the middle of your work, tie the ends together and continue crocheting, then cut and fasten off these yarns within the pillars on the reverse side of the rug. Make sure that any knots also end up on the back of the rug.

The make consists of 106 rows altogether. The pattern repeats on the rug five times, and both ends have two rows of pillars crocheted with the beige yarn. The green yarn is carried along within the pillars to the last row of pillars. Finish both short edges of the rug with a row of ss. Cut the yarn and fasten off.

▯	pillar, green
▯	pillar, beige

POSTER

SIZE	YARN	HOOK
w: 55 cm (21½ in) h: 70 cm (27½ in)	Liina fish net twine, 12-ply, off-white approx. 200 g (7 oz), black approx. 120 g (4 oz)	1.75 mm (size 6)

Positive affirmations are all over our social media accounts, and by expressing positivity to others we invite it back into our own lives in return. Everyone needs a little encouragement to live life to the max, so tie a crocheted catchphrase where it can be seen by a friend who needs a boost.

TIP!
Design your own encouraging proverb and crochet it using a pillar technique, as here, or try pixel crochet, as detailed on page 252.

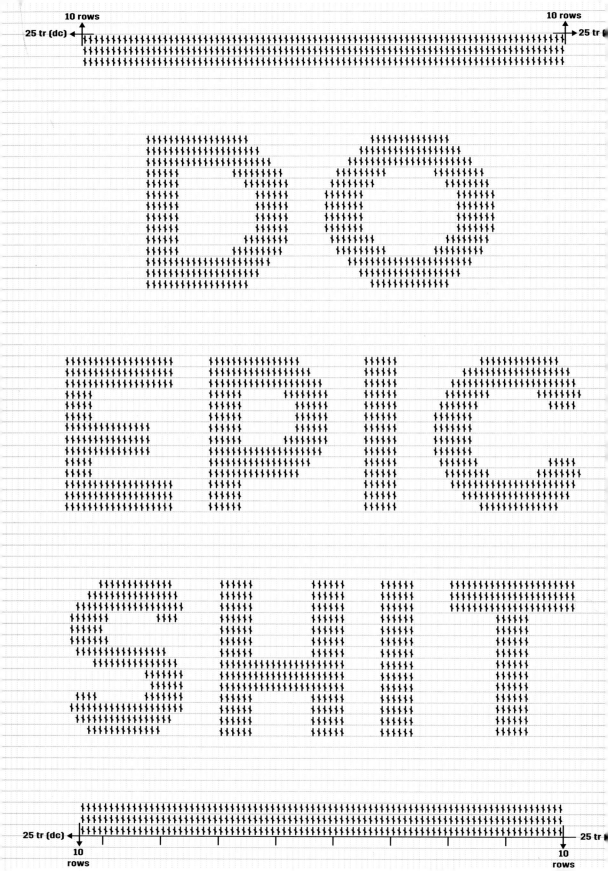

CROCHET INSTRUCTIONS

The make is crocheted back and forth using a two-colour pillar technique (see page 248 for step-by-step instructions). The non-working yarn is carried along within the pillars while working. Begin from the lower edge.

Row 1. Chain 136 stitches with the off-white yarn to begin. Crochet the first pillar into the fourth chain stitch from the hook. Carry the black yarn and work 1 treble (double) crochet stitch into each chain stitch. Crochet the last pillar in the row without the black yarn. Lightly pull on the black yarn at the end of the row to make sure it isn't left slack within the pillars. The row consists of 134 tr (dc) altogether.

Row 2. Ch 3 stitches with the off-white yarn to form the first pillar in the row. Continue by crocheting 1 tr (dc) into each pillar, putting the hook through both loops of the stitch in the row below. Carry the black yarn from the first to the penultimate pillar in the row. At the end of the row, gently pull on the carried yarn.

Rows 3–10. Crochet as for row 2. Make sure that the black yarn loop at the edges always ends up on the reverse side of the make.

Row 11. Ch 3 stitches with the off-white yarn. Crochet 23 tr (dc) and change to the black yarn on the last yoh of the following pillar. Crochet 84 tr (dc) with the black yarn, then change to the off-white yarn. Continue crocheting another 25 tr (dc) with the off-white yarn. This row sets the position of the charted design.

Rows 12–13. Crochet as for row 11.

Rows 14–19. Crochet the pillar rows with the off-white yarn while carrying the black yarn within the pillars.

Row 20. The crocheting of the text begins in this row. Continue working, following the chart. Remember to leave the black yarn loops at the edges on the reverse side of the make.

The make consists of 92 rows altogether. Cut the yarns and fasten off.

pillar, black

pillar, off-white

TYPE DESIGNER JARNO is designing fonts. Each letter is drawn by hand first, then on the computer. Jarno also likes to try out his designs on granite, using hammer and chisel to engrave the stone's surface.

SPEAKER SLIPCASE

SIZE	YARN	HOOK
w 42 cm (16½ in) h 32 cm (12⅝ in) without the lid piece	Lamana, Ica, turquoise three balls, black one ball, coral two balls. Weight of ball is 50 g (1¾ oz)	3.5 mm (E/4) and 4.5 mm (G/6)

OTHER	
Audio speaker approx. size 42 x 32 cm (16½ x 12⅝ in)	

A speaker's job is, of course, to transmit sound to the listener, but that doesn't mean it can't look good. This crocheted slipcase adds visual impact to a utilitatrian object, and looks great in the living room or home office.

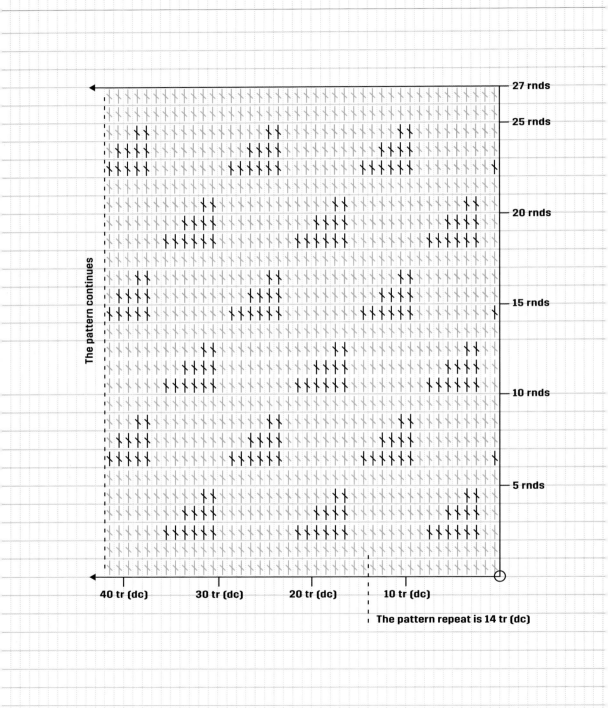

27 rnds

25 rnds

20 rnds

15 rnds

10 rnds

5 rnds

The pattern continues

40 tr (dc)   30 tr (dc)   20 tr (dc)   10 tr (dc)

The pattern repeat is 14 tr (dc)

CROCHET INSTRUCTIONS

The make is crocheted in a tube using a three-colour pillar technique, which is woked in the same way as a two-colour pillar technique (see page 246 for step-by-step instructions). All the non-working yarns are carried along within the pillars throughout.

Rnd 1. Using the 4.5 mm (G/6) hook, chain 126 stitches with the turquoise yarn to begin. Crochet loose chain stitches so they won't strain in the final make. Make sure your work isn't twisted, and close into a ring using a slip stitch. Ch 3 stitches to form the pillar of the round. Work a round of treble (double) crochet stitches, working one pillar into each chain stitch. Carry the non-working yarns along from the start. Close the round with a ss in the third chain stitch from the beginning.

Rnd 2. Crochet one round of pillars with the turquoise yarn, remembering to carry the non-working yarns within the pillars.

Rnd 3. Ch 3 stitches with the turquoise yarn to begin, carrying the non-working yarns along. Change to the black yarn on the last yarn over hook of the next pillar. Crochet 5 tr (dc) with the black yarn. Change to the coral yarn on the last yoh of the sixth pillar. Crochet 5 tr (dc) with the coral yarn. Change back to the turquoise yarn on the last yoh of the sixth pillar. The repeat pattern consists of 2 tr (dc) with the turquoise yarn, 6 tr (dc) with the black yarn and 6 tr (dc) with the coral yarn. Close the round with a ss in the third chain stitch from the start.

Rnd 4. Ch 3 stitches with the turquoise yarn. Crochet 1 tr (dc), then change to black yarn on the last yoh of the next pillar. Complete the repeat by crocheting 4 tr (dc) with black yarn and 8 tr (dc) with coral yarn. Always close the rounds with a ss in the third chain stitch from the start.

Continue crocheting, following the chart and changing to the smaller (3.5 mm/E/4) hook midway through the make so that the upper part of the slipcase will become slightly narrower to fit the speaker. The make consists of six lines of the pattern, and 25 rounds including the two turquoise pillar-rounds. Crochet another two pillar-rounds along the upper edge of the make with the turquoise yarn. Cut the yarns and fasten off.

pillar, turquoise

pillar, black

pillar, coral

UPPER EDGE LID

The lid is crocheted with the turquoise yarn using the 3.5 mm (E/4) hook.

1   For the lid, crochet 6 tr(dc)-rows worked back and forth, while decreasing the pillars from the sides. From the end of the row, where the new row begins, crochet 16 tr (dc), then put the hook through the next stitch. Catch yarn over hook and pull on the stitch, then ch another 2 stitches. These stitches form the first pillar of the lid. Continue crocheting another 51 tr (dc), then ch 2 stitches before turning. Crochet 1 tr (dc) into each pillar, then crochet 2 tr (dc) into one at the edge to decrease. To do this put the hook into the next stitch, yoh and pull through 2 loops on the hook. Repeat in the next stitch. There are now three stitches on your hook. Yoh and pull through all stitches on the hook. The first decrease is finished. **Rows 2–6.** Ch 2, 1 tr (dc) into each stitch, then crochet two pillars into one at the edge. By the end of row 6 there will be 44 tr (dc) altogether.

2   Sew the edges of the lid closed by hand. Cut the yarn and fasten off.

3   Fit the slipcase over the speaker. Be careful not to pull the case too forcefully over the speaker or it might be pulled out of shape.

4   Weave a length of yarn through alternate pillars around the bottom of the make.

5   Tighten the yarn and tie it securely. The speaker slipcase is complete.

As with all the makes you crochet for the home, you
can choose a different colour scheme than the one
detailed here, to suit the room you are accessorizing.

TUUKKA, CO-FOUNDER OF UPLOUD AUDIO, which produced the speaker used here, inspects components. Each speaker is assembled by hand and fitted into the company's self-designed casing. The case is made from an acoustically transparent material, which means that all sound frequencies pass through it unaltered. It's best to use a loosely woven cotton yarn for the crochet slipcase, to keep the sound quality just right.

BAND POSTER

SIZE	YARN	HOOK
w: 120 cm (47¼ in) h: 50 cm (19¾ in)	Liina fish net twine, 12-ply, off-white 600 g (21 oz)	1.75 mm (size 6)

Yes, you can combine granny-chic and death metal – or your preferred musical genre – by crocheting your favourite band's logo in mammoth size. Why not fix it to a pole and roll it up in your festival kit? You will soon be the envy of busloads of fans, all eager to be taught the secrets of logo-crocheting.

TIP!
You can adapt this pixel crochet project to your preferred band's logo. Use a pencil to draw the logo in pixel form onto graph paper. Choose an appropriate hook and yarn – firm cotton is a good choice – and crochet a test piece of 10 x 10 squares. Measure the size of the test piece to approximate the final size of your finished make.

180 squares   170 squares   160 squares   150 squares   140 squares   130 squares   120 squares

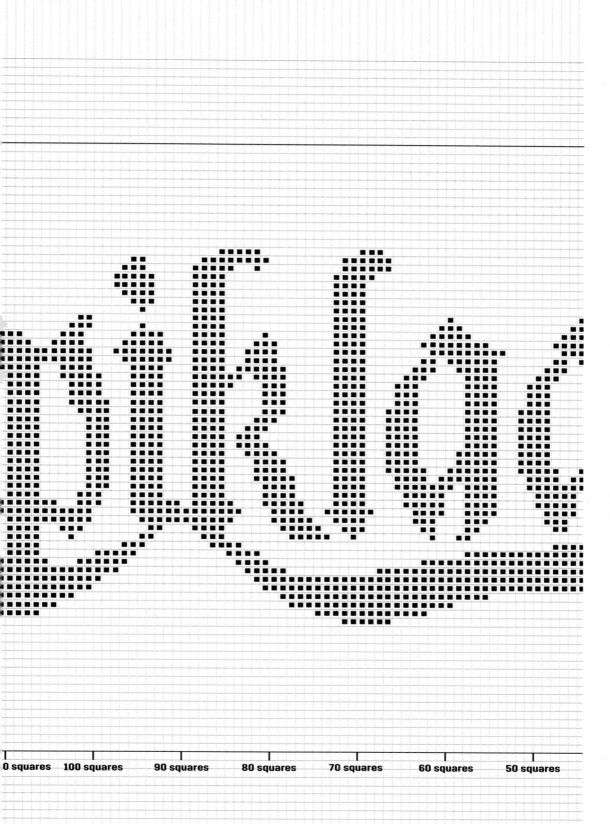

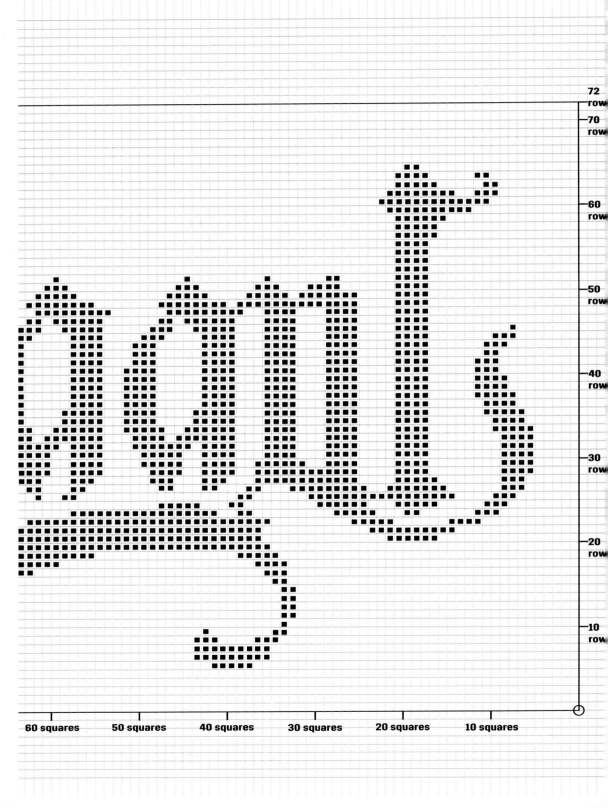

72
row

70
row

60
row

50
row

40
row

30
row

20
row

10
row

60 squares   50 squares   40 squares   30 squares   20 squares   10 squares

CROCHET INSTRUCTIONS

The make is worked as a pixel crochet (see page 252 for step-by-step instructions). Start crocheting from the bottom up.

Row 1. Chain 365 stitches to begin. Catch the yarn over hook and crochet the first pillar into the seventh stitch from the hook. You have now made one square. Ch 1 stitch, miss (skip) one stitch then work 1 treble (double) crochet stitch. Repeat to the end of the row. The row consists of 180 squares altogether. If you find you have too many stitches you can simply unravel the unwanted chain stitches, leaving one stitch for finishing. The rest of your work won't unravel because chain stitches will lock while crocheting. If your work contains too few stitches, continue crocheting chain stitches using the yarn end.

Row 2. Ch 4 then turn. Catch yoh and crochet 1 tr (dc) into the previous row's pillar. Put the hook through both loops of the stitch in the row below. Crochet 1 tr (dc) into each pillar, and always chain 1 stitch in between the pillars. At the end of the row, crochet 1 tr (dc) into the second stitch of the ch-arch. The row consists of 180 squares altogether.

Rows 3–5. Crochet as for row 2.

Row 6. This row will begin crocheting the pixel pattern. Crochet the first pixel into the 38th square from the edge. To make the pixel, crochet a pillar into the previous row's pillar, plus a pillar into the previous row's chain stitch that was crocheted in between the pillars, plus yet another pillar into next pillar in the previous row. One pixel is finished. If there is only one pixel at this point, continue by crocheting squares. If the pattern continues with several pixels, then continue by crocheting pillars without adding chain stitches in between. Count the pixel spaces carefully to avoid having to unravel your progress. There are five faulty pixels in my finished Korpiklaani poster, but due to the asymmetry of the logo the mistakes don't show in the finished make.

Continue by following the chart.

Keep checking that the work is 180 squares wide. The finished project contains 72 rows altogether. Cut the yarn and fasten off.

■ pixel

□ square

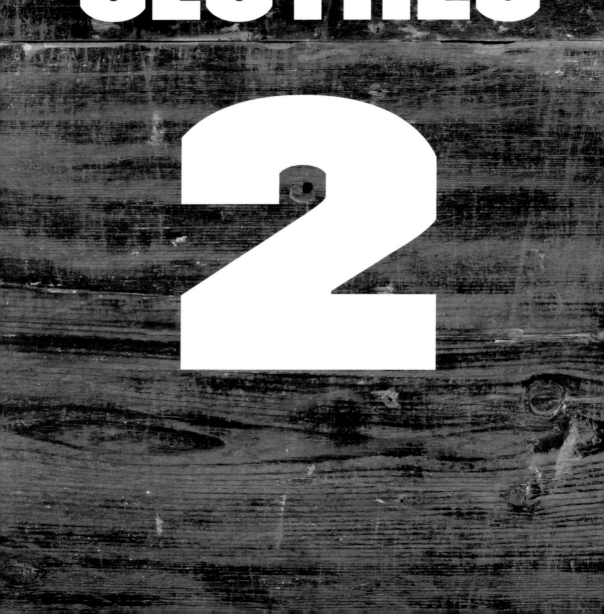

CLOTHES

2

WAYFARER'S JUMPER

SIZE	YARN	HOOK
This will change according to your choice of yarn. Here, the size is men's M	Gepard, Sømand's Garn, dark blue three skeins, grey three skeins. Weight of skein is 150 g (5 oz)	4.0 mm (G/6)

OTHER	
Small leather breast pocket	

This crocheted jumper of coarse Icelandic wool is so manly you can imagine it smoking a pipe in the wardrobe all by its lonesome. In spring the jumper can be simply worn over a short-sleeved T-shirt, and in winter it will slip underneath a jacket to keep the wearer cosy and warm. My father wore the jumper as he went to chop firewood on a chilly June evening in Northern Karelia.

1

2

The wayfarer's jumper is crocheted in a spiral tube, starting from the top and working downward. Begin crocheting from the neckline, working the top part as a rectangle until you reach the armpits. At the beginning of the work, always add stitches on the four corners of each round until the make is the desired size. The body and sleeves are then worked separately.

1   **Rnd 1.** Chain 112 stitches with the dark blue yarn to begin. Aim to chain loose stitches so they won't strain in the final make. Make sure your work isn't twisted and join the stitches in a ring using a slip stitch. Ch 4 stitches; the first three of the chs will form the first pillar of the round and the fourth will be a corner. Work 1 treble (double) crochet stitch in the beginning stitch, then go on to crochet 21 tr (dc). Crochet 1 ch and 1 tr (dc) into the same stitch as the previous tr (dc). Crochet 34 tr (dc), then crochet 1 tr (dc), 1 ch and 1 tr (dc) into the next stitch. Crochet 20 tr (dc), then crochet 1 tr (dc), 1 ch and 1 tr (dc) into the next stitch. Crochet another 34 tr (dc). Close the round with a ss in the third chain stitch from the beginning, making the slip stitch's yarn over hook with the grey yarn.

    Rnd 2. Ch 4 with the grey yarn to begin; these chs work in the same way as those at the start of round 1. Do not carry the non-working yarn; bring it back into the work at the changeover point. Crochet 1 tr (dc) into the previous round's corner chain stitch, then continue crocheting 1 tr (dc) into every pillar. At the next corner, crochet 1 tr (dc), 1 ch and another tr (dc) into the same chain stitch. By adding pillars in this way into the four corners of each round, the work will increase evenly. Crochet 38 tr (dc) into the front and back pieces of this round, 24 tr (dc) on the sleeves. At the end of the round, crochet the last tr (dc) into the same place where the chain stitches are situated in the beginning. Close the round with a ss, and yoh with the dark blue yarn.

Rnd 3. Work as for rnd 2. Crochet 1 tr (dc), 1 ch and 1 tr (dc) into each corner of the round. The round is always closed with a ss in the third chain stitch from the start. Catch the slip stitch's yoh with a new colour. Continue crocheting the work in the same way. Crochet 25 rounds, or as many as needed until the work is the right size on the rectangular top part. Do not cut the yarns. Check the jumper for size by pulling it on and measuring that the body and sleeve openings are big enough. The jumper should be a little loose in both the body and the sleeves. At this point the top piece should have 168 tr (dc) and both sleeve openings should have 70 tr (dc). Unravel or add rounds as needed. Fold the work in half with the right side facing out. Next, crochet the body of the jumper in the round, starting from the armpits at the round's changeover point.

2   With the grey thread, ch 3 stitches in the corner chain stitch to form the first pillar of the round. Continue by crocheting 1 tr (dc) into each pillar. At the body's second armpit, crochet 1 tr (dc) into each of the two chain stitches, then continue working in the round. There will be a small gap in the armpit, which will be sewn shut by hand at the end. Close the round with a ss in the third chain stitch from the start, making the yoh with the dark blue yarn. At the end of the round, the work contains 170 tr (dc) in total, with 2 + 2 tr (dc) are added in the corners. After this there is no need to add pillars into the body. The work is crocheted to the desired length by changing the yarn colours on each round. The body of the jumper contains 34 rounds in total. Crochet one round of dc (sc) and finish the edge with a ss-round. Cut the yarn and fasten off.

SLEEVES

3 Begin crocheting the sleeves as for the body.
Crochet 1 tr (dc) into each pillar with the grey
yarn, close the round with a ss into the third
chain stitch from the beginning, yoh with the
dark blue yarn. At the end of the round there
are 70 tr (dc) in total.

Rnd 2. Ch 3 stitches, crochet the next
2 tr (dc) together. Continue by crocheting
1 tr (dc) into each pillar and close the round
with a ss.

Rnd 3. Work a tr(dc)-round with the grey yarn.

Rnd 4. Crochet a tr(dc)-round with the dark
blue yarn and crochet the last two pillars of
the round together. Only decrease the sleeves
while using the dark blue yarn, one decrease
per round: the decreases are worked at the
end of every other round, and the beginning of
the alternating rounds.

Repeat rnds 3–4 to rnd 39. After the decrease
rounds, crochet another 13 rounds without
any decreases, keeping the stripe pattern
correct, or as many rounds as needed until
the sleeves are the desired length. Crochet 1
dc(sc)-round at the edge of the sleeve, then
finish with a round of ss. Cut the yarns and
fasten off. Work the other sleeve following the
same instructions.

NECKLINE

4 Crochet 4 tr(dc)-rows back and forth on the back part of the neckline. Begin crocheting the rows from the right side of the neckline and crochet 1 tr (dc) into each pillar.

5 Ch 2, attach ch-arch to the edge of the neckline with a ss and turn work. Crochet 1 tr (dc) into the same stitch, then continue crocheting pillars. At the end of the row, crochet 2 tr (dc) at the same spot. Ch 2, attach to the edge of the neckline with a ss and turn work. Crochet four rows in total following the same instructions, always adding 1 tr (dc) to the edges of the rows. After the fourth row, ch 1 stitch then turn. Crochet a dc(sc)-round around the edge of the neckline, working 1 dc (sc) into each pillar. Finish the edge with a round of ss, cut the yarn and fasten off.

6 Sew a leather chest pocket onto the front of the jumper with a strong sewing thread. You might also want to attach leather elbow patches to make the jumper more hardwearing.

7 The wayfarer's jumper is complete.

ANCHOR POCKET

SIZE	YARN	HOOK
w: 15 cm (6 in)	A small amount of Liina fish	1.75 mm
h: 17 cm (6¾ in)	net twine, yellow and blue	(size 6)

OTHER	
Button	

Crocheting this little anchor pocket won't take long, and you only need a small ball of yarn. A buttonhole is crocheted at the mouth of the pocket, and the pocket and button are sewn onto the T-shirt. The make is crocheted back and forth using a two-colour pillar technique (see page 248 for step-by-step instructions).

Row 1. Chain 40 stitches with the yellow yarn to begin. Work 1 treble (double) stitch into the fourth stitch from the hook, carry the blue yarn and crochet a tr(dc)-row. Drop the blue yarn one pillar from the end of the row. The row contains 38 tr (dc) in total. **Rows 2–4.** Always ch 3 stitches to begin, carry blue yarn and crochet a tr(dc)-row. Always drop blue yarn one pillar from the end of the row. Remember to drop the blue yarn on the wrong side of the work at both edges of the row. **Row 5.** Work 12 tr (dc) yellow, 14 tr (dc) blue, 12 tr (dc) yellow. **Row 6.** Crochet 9 tr (dc) yellow, 20 tr (dc) blue, 9 tr (dc) yellow. **Row 7.** Crochet 7 tr (dc) yellow, 6 tr (dc) blue, 4 tr (dc) yellow, 4 tr (dc) blue, 4 tr (dc) yellow, 6 tr (dc) blue, 7 tr (dc) yellow. **Row 8.** Crochet 6 tr (dc) yellow, 4 tr (dc) blue, 7 tr (dc) yellow, 4 tr (dc) blue, 7 tr (dc) yellow, 4 tr (dc) blue, 6 tr (dc) yellow. **Rows 9–10.** Crochet 5 tr (dc) yellow, 3 tr (dc) blue, 9 tr (dc) yellow, 4 tr (dc) blue, 9 tr (dc) yellow, 3 tr (dc) blue, 5 tr (dc) yellow. **Row 11.** Crochet 17 tr (dc) yellow, 4 tr (dc) blue, 17 tr (dc) yellow. **Row 12.** Crochet 12 tr (dc) yellow, 14 tr (dc) blue, 12 tr (dc) yellow. **Rows 13–14.** Work as for row 11. **Row 15.** Crochet 15 tr (dc) yellow, 8 tr (dc) blue, 15 tr (dc) yellow. **Row 16.** Crochet 14 tr (dc) yellow, 3 tr (dc) blue, 4 tr (dc) yellow, 3 tr (dc) blue, 14 tr (dc) yellow. **Row 17.** Crochet 13 tr (dc) yellow, 3 tr (dc) blue, 6 tr (dc) yellow, 3 tr (dc) blue, 13 tr (dc) yellow. **Row 18.** Work as for row 16. **Row 19.** Work as for row 15. **Rows 20–22.** Crochet yellow tr(dc)-rows.

Crochet a dc(sc)-round around the edge of the pocket. Ch a few stitches along the upper edge to make a buttonhole, as for Steps 4–5 of the can carrier on page 159. Measure the length of the buttonhole by measuring against your chosen button. Cut the yarns and fasten off. Sew pocket onto T-shirt.

FINGERLESS MITTENS

SIZE	YARN	HOOK
This will change according to your choice of yarn	Madelinetosh, Sock, one skein. Weight of skein is approx. 100 g (3½ oz). Wool yarn for the thumb	3.5 mm (E/4)

Woollen fingerless mittens are a useful addition to the kitbag of the adventurous photographer, or any outdoorsy type who needs warm hands as well as fingertip sensitivity. You can use the same instructions to make different sizes, simply by changing the yarn: a thin yarn for small mittens and a thick or doubled yarn for larger ones. You can also crochet a thumb using leftover yarn.

WRIST PIECE

1   Wind the yarn into two similarly sized balls and use one strand from each ball held together. Chain 16 stitches. Put the hook through the second stitch from the hook and crochet a row of double (single) crochet stitches: 15 dc (sc) in total. Ch 1, then turn. Crochet 1 dc (sc) into each stitch, putting the hook through only the back loop of each stitch. There are 38 ribbed rows in total. Find the step-by-step instructions for ribbed crochet on page 250.

2   At the end of the last cuff row, put the hook through the edge stitch in the first row and catch the loop of the last stitch.

3   Crochet the short seam closed using slip stitches.

HAND PIECE

4   Ch 3 to form the first pillar of the round.

5   In the first round of the hand piece, work 1 treble (double) crochet stitch into the end of each row. Close the round with a ss in the third chain stitch from the beginning. The round contains 39 tr (dc) in total.

6   Ch 3 stitches at the beginning of each round.

7   Continue by working 1 tr (dc) crochet stitch into each stitch, inserting the hook under both loops. Depending on the desired size of the hand piece, crochet four to five rounds before starting on the thumb.

8   In this round, you will crochet the opening for the thumb. Ch 3 and crochet 9 tr (dc) to begin the round.

9   Work 8 dc (sc), miss (skip) eight pillars and fasten the ch-arch to the ninth pillar. Continue by crocheting pillars.

10 Next round, crochet 1 tr (dc) into each stitch of the ch-arch. Continue by crocheting pillars.

11 After the thumb opening, crochet another four rounds of pillars.

12 Finish the upper edge of the work with an ss-round. Cut the yarns and fasten off. Crochet another identical mitten, but with the thumb opening on the right side of the hand piece this time: ch 3 and crochet 20 tr (dc), then 8 dc (sc), miss (skip) 8 stitches and work 10 more tr (dc).

THUMB

13 The thumb is crocheted using dc (sc) stitches and one strand of yarn. Crochet 8 dc (sc) along the lower edge of the thumb opening, working 1 dc (sc) into each pillar. Put the hook through both loops of each pillar.

14 Crochet 1–3 dc (sc), depending on the desired thumb size, into the pillars on the short edge of the thumb opening. Crochet another 1–3 dc (sc) into each pillar on the top: crochet 1 dc (sc) into each pillar for a woman's size, and 3 dc (sc) into each pillar for a man's size. The thumb opening will consist of 18–22 dc (sc) in total. Crochet 7–8 dc(sc)-rounds for the thumb. Finish the edge with a ss-round. Cut the yarn and fasten off. The fingerless mittens are finished.

THE FINGERLESS MITTENS HERE are made using Madelinetosh Sock yarn worked double. The mittens worn on page 82 are also crocheted using double yarn but out of the slightly thicker Sport wool. The ladies' mittens are a size smaller, although they were both worked according to the same instructions.

NECK WARMER

SIZE	YARN	HOOK
l: 50 cm (19¾ in) h: 24 cm (9½ in)	Millamia, Naturally Soft Merino, blue two balls, beige two balls, green one ball. Weight of ball is 50 g (1¾ oz)	2.5 mm (B/1)

OTHER	
Zip (zipper) that opens all the way l: 22 cm (8¾ in)	

A scarf with a zip (zipper) is a real all-round warmer. This scarf is sporty and practical and can be worked in only a few evenings. Sew the zip (zipper) on with a sewing machine or by hand; just remember to choose a zip (zipper) that opens all the way.

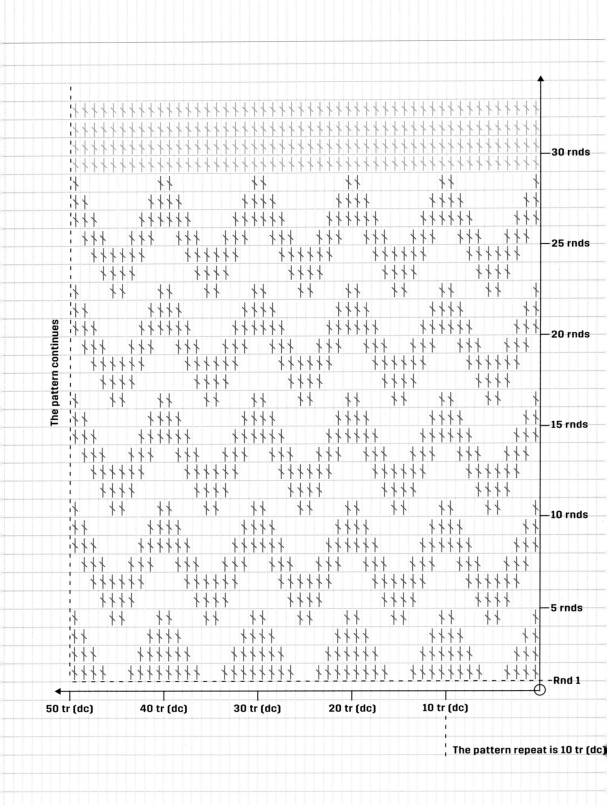

The pattern continues

30 rnds

25 rnds

20 rnds

15 rnds

10 rnds

5 rnds

Rnd 1

50 tr (dc)   40 tr (dc)   30 tr (dc)   20 tr (dc)   10 tr (dc)

The pattern repeat is 10 tr (dc)

CROCHET INSTRUCTIONS

The work is crocheted using a two-colour pillar technique worked in a tube (see page 246 for step-by-step instructions). Carry the non-working yarn along within the pillars while crocheting.

Rnd 1. Chain 120 stitches with the blue yarn to begin, chaining loose stitches so they won't strain in the final make. Check that your work isn't twisted, then close it into a ring using a slip stitch. Work a round of double (single) crochet: 1 ch to begin, then 1 dc (sc) into each chain stitch. Carry the beige yarn from the beginning. Close the round with a ss into the first chain stitch.

Rnd 2. Ch 3 stitches with the blue yarn to form the first pillar of the round. Carry the beige yarn and crochet 2 tr (dc) with the blue yarn. Change to the beige yarn on the last yarn over hook of the third pillar. Crochet 1 tr (dc) with the beige yarn, then change back to the blue yarn on the last yoh of the second pillar. The pattern repeat consists of eight blue pillars and two beige pillars in total. Crochet four pillars with the blue yarn at the end of the round. Close the round with a ss in the third chain stitch from the start.

Rnd 3. Ch 3 stitches to begin. Work 1 treble (double) crochet stitch with the blue yarn, then change to the beige yarn on the last yoh of the second pillar. The pattern repeat consists of 4 tr (dc) with the beige yarn, and 6 tr (dc) with the blue yarn. The rounds are always closed with a ss in the third chain stitch from the start. Continue working, following the chart up to rnd 29. Rnds 30–37 are worked entirely in the green yarn. Unwind a small piece from the green ball into a separate ball. This yarn will be carried within the pillars as in the patterned section. Crochet 1 tr (dc) into each pillar for eight rounds in total.

Rnd 38. Crochet the same pattern as for rnds 2–29. The pattern is crocheted as a mirror image, so the first round is the same as rnd 29 on the chart.

Crochet a round of dc (sc) stitches along the edge of the last round, using the blue yarn. These dc(sc)-rounds at the edges of the neck warmer make it easier to sew on the zip (zipper). Cut the yarns and fasten off.

Lay the tube flat. Separate the zip (zipper) into two pieces. Pin one piece to the back of the dc (sc) rounds at the start and finish of the neck warmer. Make sure that the changeover points of the rounds end up at the bottom edge of the work, and that the zigzag pattern lines up on both sides of the zip (zipper). From the right side, carefully sew the zip (zipper) in place between the layers, taking care not to stretch the edges.

pillar, blue	
pillar, beige	
pillar, green	

BOW TIE

SIZE	YARN	HOOK
w: 11 cm (4⅜ in) h: 5 cm (2 in)	Maharaja silk yarn, approx. 20 g (¾ oz)	1.25 mm (size 10)

OTHER		
Old bow tie, piece of leather belt		

A bow tie crocheted in a silk yarn can be casually worn at an informal summer party, or make it up in a wool yarn to warm up the winter office look. If you need to rustle up a formal bow tie at the last minute, don't worry about the strap, simply attach the tie to the shirt collar with a safety pin.

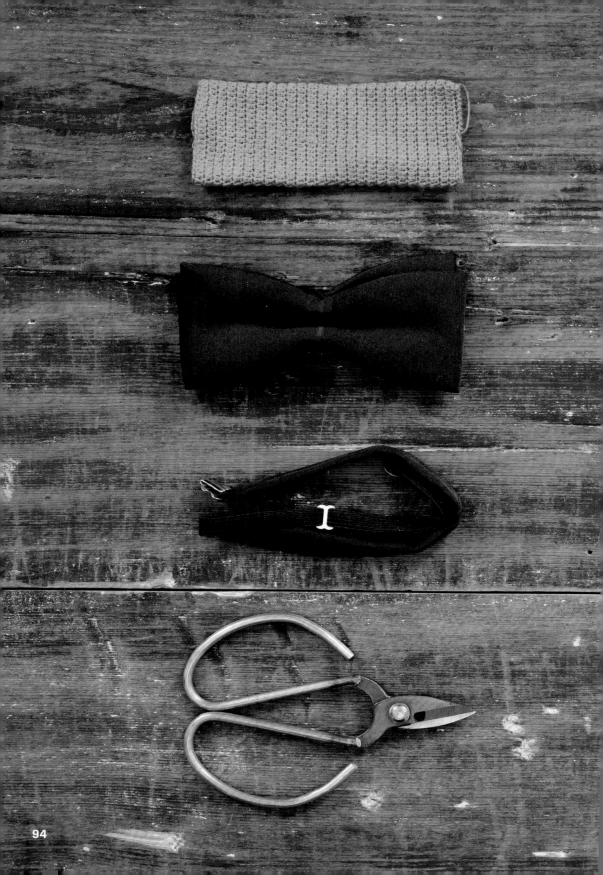

1 The work is crocheted in a tube using a pillar technique (see page 240 for step-by-step instructions). Chain a round of stitches to begin and close into a ring using a slip stitch. The number of stitches you chain will determine the height of your bow tie: both bows here start with 45 chain stitches. Using the red silk the tie is 5 cm (2 in) high, while the same amount of stitches in the green wool (opposite) make it 7 cm (2¾ in) high.

Rnd 1. Ch 3 stitches to form the first pillar of each round. Work 1 treble (double) crochet stitch into each chain stitch, then close the round with a ss in the third chain stitch from the beginning.

Rnds 2–the end. Ch 3 stitches, then crochet 1 tr (dc) into each stitch. Close with a ss in the third chain stitch from the beginning. Continue crocheting tr(dc)-rounds until the bow is the desired width. The width of the silk bow is 11 cm (4⅜ in), and the work contains 27 rounds in total. The width of the wool bow is 13 cm (5⅛ in), and the work contains 20 rounds in total. Sew the ends closed using small stitches.

2   Measure the mid-point of the bow, fold it in half, then slip a long needle through it. Sew the bow closed in the middle with a few stitches.

3   Punch holes through both ends of the piece of leather belt ready for sewing.

4   Remove the bow from an old bow tie and iron the neck strap smooth. Position the leather piece and the neck strap in the middle, on each side of the bow.

5   Sew the leather piece tightly closed with strong thread. Make sure you don't sew the leather piece onto the neck strap. The leather loop should move freely along the strap so the tie can be slid into the right place to suit the collar.

6   The bow tie is finished.

TIP!
You'll only need a little yarn to crochet the bow tie, so why not use leftover yarn? This green bow tie was made using thin merino wool.

YOUNG HUSKY SIBLINGS MÄYRÄ AND AHMA have made it into the cottage and onto the hearth. Huskies are a kind breed and great company, but they are also especially active, and like to move. It was nearly impossible to get the siblings to sit still during the photo shoot. When one would look into the camera, the other's bow tie would have spun out of place. They slunk out into the crisp summer evening straight after the shoot.

SLIPPERS

SIZE	YARN	HOOK
This will change according to your choice of yarn. Here, the size is men's 9 (10)	Putkis hollow yarn, melange green approx. 300 g (10½ oz)	5.0 mm (H/8)

OTHER	
Wool insoles	

What better way to warm your feet in the comfort of your own home than with a pair of wool-lined slippers? Slippers crocheted using a thin yarn will keep their shape in the wash, as long as you take out the wool insoles first. Slippers are an excellent substitute for woolly socks, and can be crocheted in sizes to fit the whole family.

The toe of the slipper is worked in a tube using double (single) crochet and increasing stitches at both edges. The body is worked back and forth while increasing in the middle. The heel is crocheted last and worked back and forth.

THE TOE

1 **Rnd 1.** Make a slip knot on the hook, then chain 2 stitches. Crochet 8 dc (sc) into the first chain stitch. Move seamlessly to the second round in a spiral.

Rnd 2. Crochet 2 dc (sc) into each stitch, making 16 dc (sc) in total for this round.

Rnd 3. Crochet 5 dc (sc) into the next stitch. Crochet 1 dc (sc) into the next seven stitches, then crochet 5 dc (sc) into the following stitch. Crochet 1 dc (sc) into the next seven stitches. There are 24 dc (sc) in total for this round. The increase stitches will be on both sides of the toe piece.

2 **Rnd 4.** Crochet 1 dc (sc) into the next two stitches, then crochet 3 dc (sc) into the next stitch. The increase will settle in the middle of the five-dc(sc)-group in the previous round. Crochet 1 dc (sc) into the next 11 stitches, then crochet 3 dc (sc) into the next stitch. Crochet 1 dc (sc) into the next 11 stitches. The round consists of 28 dc (sc) in total.

Rnd 5. Work as for the previous round, but crochet 2 dc (sc) in the middle of the previous round's three-dc(sc)-group on both sides; crochet 1 dc (sc) in the other stitches. The round consists of 30 dc (sc) in total.

Rnd 6. Crochet a dc(sc)-round without any increases.

3 **Rnd 7.** Crochet 2 dc (sc) in the middle of the previous round's increase-groups, on both sides; crochet 1 dc (sc) in the other stitches.

Rnds 8–10. Crochet a dc(sc)-round without any increases.

Rnd 11. Crochet 2 dc (sc) in the middle of the previous round's increase-groups, on both sides; crochet 1 dc (sc) in the other stitches.

Rnds 12–14. Crochet dc(sc)-rounds without any increases.

Rnd 15. Crochet 2 dc (sc) in the middle of the previous round's increase-groups, on both sides; crochet 1 dc (sc) on the other stitches. The round consists of 36 dc (sc) in total.

Rnds 16–17. Crochet dc(sc)-rounds without increases. Measure the size of the slipper at this point, and add or remove rounds according to your size. If the toe of the slipper is too loose, remove increase stitches from the earlier rounds.

THE BODY

4 **Row 18.** Begin at the round's start point and crochet 22 dc (sc), then crochet 1 ch and turn. Continue working back and forth.

5 **Row 19.** Crochet 1 dc (sc) into the next 21 stitches; the beginning chain counts as the first stitch of the row. Leave the remaining 14 stitches of the toe unworked.

Rows 20–35. Crochet rows back and forth without increases.

Row 36. Crochet 2 dc (sc) on both sides of the body, eight dc (sc) from the edges: crochet 1 dc (sc) in the other stitches.

Row 37. Crochet a dc(sc)-row without any increases.

Row 38. Crochet 2 dc (sc) on both sides of the body, nine dc (sc) from the edges: crochet 1 dc (sc) in the other stitches.

Rows 39–41. Crochet dc(sc)-rows without any increases.

8 Crochet the heel piece to the slip stitches on the seam, stitch by stitch.

9 Cut the yarn and fasten off. Turn the slipper right side out so the heel seam is inside.

10 Crochet a row of dc (sc) stitches around the edge of the slipper. You might want to crochet this border with a smaller hook and a bit more tightly, so that the slipper will mould to the foot and stay on while walking. Finish the edge with a row of ss. Cut the yarn and fasten off.

11 The slipper is complete. Crochet a second slipper by following the same instructions.

THE HEEL

6 **Row 42.** Continue by crocheting the 9 dc (sc) stitches of the heel back and forth: ch 1 stitch, then turn and crochet 8 dc (sc). The beginning chain is included in the stitch count.

7 **Rows 43–49.** Crochet dc(sc)-rows. Take out the hook but do not cut the yarn. Turn the slipper inside out. Put the hook through the corner of the body opposite the heel piece and catch the last stitch made on the hook.

FIVE YEAR-OLD NOAK BUILDS LEGO SLIPPERS.
Slippers crocheted with double wool yarn are still slightly too big for such little feet, but the wool insoles give them a better fit. Fasten some Lego blocks onto the toes by first drilling little holes into them and then sewing them on. These Lego slippers will have the biggest sleepyhead happily tiptoeing to the breakfast table.

CHILD'S SLIPPERS

SIZE
Child's size 9.5 (10)

YARN
Cascade Heathers, dark blue, one skein
approx. 100 g (3½ oz). The slippers are
crocheted with two-ply yarn

HOOK
4.5 mm (G/6)

OTHER
Wool insoles

To work the child's slipper, follow the instructions on page 103 to rnd 4.

Rnd 5. Crochet 1 dc(sc)-round without increases.

Rnd 6. Crochet 2 dc (sc) in the middle of the previous round's increase-groups, on both sides; crochet 1 dc (sc) in the other stitches.

Rnds 7–9. Crochet dc(sc)-rounds.

Rnd 10. Crochet 2 dc (sc) in the middle of the previous round's increase-groups, on both sides; crochet 1 dc (sc) in the other stitches.

Rnds 11–13. Crochet dc(sc)-rounds.

Rnd 14. Crochet 2 dc (sc) in the middle of the previous round's increase-groups, on both sides; crochet 1 dc (sc) in the other stitches.

Rnds 15–17. Crochet dc(sc)-rounds.

Row 18. Work the body as for row 19 of the man's slipper, but leave the remaining 12 stitches of the toe unworked.

Rows 19–30. Crochet rows back and forth.

Row 31. Crochet 2 dc (sc) on both sides of the body, six stitches from the edges; crochet 1 dc (sc) in the other stitches.

Row 32. Crochet a dc(sc)-row.

Row 33. Crochet as for row 31.

Rows 34–35. Crochet dc(sc)-rows.

Next, crochet the heel of the slipper following the instructions on page 104: the width of the heel is 7 dc (sc). Crochet eight rows for the heel. Slip stitch the heel closed, cut the yarn and fasten off. Crochet a row of dc (sc) stitches around the edge and finish it with a row of slip stitches. Follow the same instructions to crochet the second slipper. You can change the size of the slipper by adding or removing rows from the body. Your choice of yarn and personal crochet tension will also influence the final size of the slipper.

WOMAN'S SLIPPERS

SIZE
Woman's size 6 (8½)

YARN
Putkis, coral approx. 80 g (2¾ oz) and off-white approx. 180 g (6¼ oz)

HOOK
6.0 mm (J/10)

To crochet the woman's slippers, follow the instructions on page 103 to rnd 6, beginning with the coral yarn.

Rnd 7. Crochet a dc(sc)-round without increases.

Rnd 8. Crochet 2 dc (sc) in the middle of the previous round's increase-groups, on both sides; crochet 1 dc (sc) in the other stitches.

Rnds 9–11. Crochet dc(sc)-rounds.

Rnd 12. This round will change colour. Crochet half the round then change to the off-white yarn; the colour change will be on the bottom of the slipper. Continue by crocheting dc (sc) stitches.

Rnds 13–15. Crochet dc(sc)-rounds.

Row 16. Work the body as for the man's slipper, but leave the remaining 12 stitches of the toe unworked.

Rows 17–30. Crochet rows back and forth.

Row 31. Crochet 2 dc (sc) on both sides of the body, seven stitches from the edges; crochet 1 dc (sc) in the other stitches.

Row 32. Crochet a dc(sc)-row.

Row 33. Crochet as for row 31.

Rows 34–36. Crochet dc(sc)-rows.

Next, crochet the heel of the slipper by following the instructions for the man's slipper. The width of the heel of the woman's slipper is 8 dc (sc). Crochet eight rows, slip stitch the heel closed then cut the yarn and fasten off. Crochet a row of dc (sc) stitches around the edge and finish it with a row of slip stitches. Follow the same instructions to crochet the second slipper. You can change the size of the slipper by adding or removing rows from the body. Your choice of yarn and personal crochet tension will also influence the final size of the slipper.

BOWLER HAT

SIZE	YARN	HOOK
This will change according to your choice of yarn. The inner diameter shown here is approx. 20 cm (8 in)	Adriafil, Rafia frond thread four skeins. Weight of skein is 25 g (1 oz)	6.0 mm (J/10)

If only someone had thought to crochet a bowler hat in Charlie Chaplin's day, it could well have been his summer favourite. The British bowler may have all but disappeared from the high street, but I want to bring it back into fashion. This stretchy hat fits on the back of the head without damaging the hairdo, and suits just about anyone.

TIP!
You can crochet a winter bowler using a thicker yarn, but you will need to miss a few rounds to achieve a snug fit.

1 **Rnd 1.** Crochet the bowler using two strands of yarn held together. Make a slip knot on the hook, then chain 2 stitches.

2 Work 9 double (single) crochet stitches into the second chain stitch from the hook. Move seamlessly to the next round in a spiral.

3 **Rnd 2.** Crochet 2 dc (sc) into every stitch. The round consists of 18 dc (sc) in total.

4 **Rnd 3.** Crochet 2 dc (sc) into every other stitch; crochet 1 dc (sc) in the intervening stitches: 27 dc (sc) in total.
Rnd 4. Crochet 2 dc (sc) into every third stitch; crochet 1 dc (sc) in the intervening stitches: 36 dc (sc) in total.
Rnd 5. Crochet a dc(sc)-round without any increases.

5 **Rnd 6.** Crochet 2 dc (sc) into every fourth stitch; crochet 1 dc (sc) in the intervening stitches: 45 dc (sc) in total.

Rnd 7. Crochet 2 dc (sc) into every fifth stitch; crochet 1 dc (sc) in the intervening stitches: 54 dc (sc) in total.
Rnd 8. Crochet 1 dc (sc) into every sixth stitch; crochet 1 dc (sc) in the intervening stitches: 63 dc (sc) in total.
Rnds 9–21. Crochet dc(sc)-rounds.
Rnd 22. The brim. Crochet 2 dc (sc) into every other stitch; crochet 1 dc (sc) in the intervening stitches.
Rnds 23–25. Crochet dc(sc)-rounds. Finish the edge with a round of slip stitches. Cut the yarn and fasten off.

6 The bowler hat is complete. Try the hat on now and again while crocheting. Your choice of yarn and personal crochet tension will influence the final size of the work. If the bowler is too small, add stitches to rnd 9. If it is too big, remove the increase stitches on rnd 8. You can crochet this bowler in a single evening.

CERAMIC ARTIST LAURA is teaching photojournalist Miikka to crochet pillars out of thick Moppari-cord. Laura is wearing a bowler hat crocheted using Raffia-wood fibre; the bowler is not exclusively a man's hat. On her wrist, Laura wears a bracelet of crocheted chain (see page 188), made using red Petra-yarn with a 1.5 mm (size 8) hook. There are 14 links in the bracelet, and the fastening is a lobster clasp.

T-SHIRT SCARF

SIZE
h: 50 cm (19¾ in)
circumference: 80 cm (31½ in)

OTHER
Two old T-shirts

Repurposing old clothes is cathartic and creative. All sorts of textiles can be reused: denim is great for hardwearing items for the home; a tatty jumper can find new life as a hat, or two; and if a hole appears in your favourite T-shirt, you can cut the arms off and turn it into a tube scarf. In this project, two much-loved band T-shirts have been combined. The photo shows Unto, vocalist with Helsinki band Rytmihäiriö, wearing the finished scarf that bears his band's name.

Wash and iron two old T-shirts. Lay one T-shirt flat and measure an area 45 cm (17¾ in) wide, with the logo centred within that area. Cut through both layers (front and back) cutting away the sides and sleeves. Cut the length to include the whole logo. Cut the second T-shirt to the same width and length, again keeping the logo centred.

1 Put the two pieces of one T-shirt right sides together and sew the side seams. Do the same with the other T-shirt pieces. Right sides together, nest the shirt pieces inside each other, with the side seams aligned.

2 Sew the pieces to each other around the upper edge, taking a 1 cm (⅜ in) seam allowance.

3 Turn the work right side out. On both layers, turn under a narrow hem all around the bottom edge and pin then sew the layers together close to the edge. You can also sew the bottom edge closed without turning under a hem. The T-shirt fabric will roll up slightly at the edges if you stretch them a little.

4 Press the scarf and the upper and lower edges. The tube scarf is complete.

PASSPORT BAG

SIZE	YARN	HOOK
w: 24 cm (9½ in) h: 15 cm (6 in)	Schachenmayr, Catania Grande, grey two balls. Weight of ball is 50 g (1¾ oz)	3.5 mm (E/4)

OTHER	
Zip (zipper) l: 20 cm (8 in), leather strap l: 15 cm (6 in), small lobster clasp	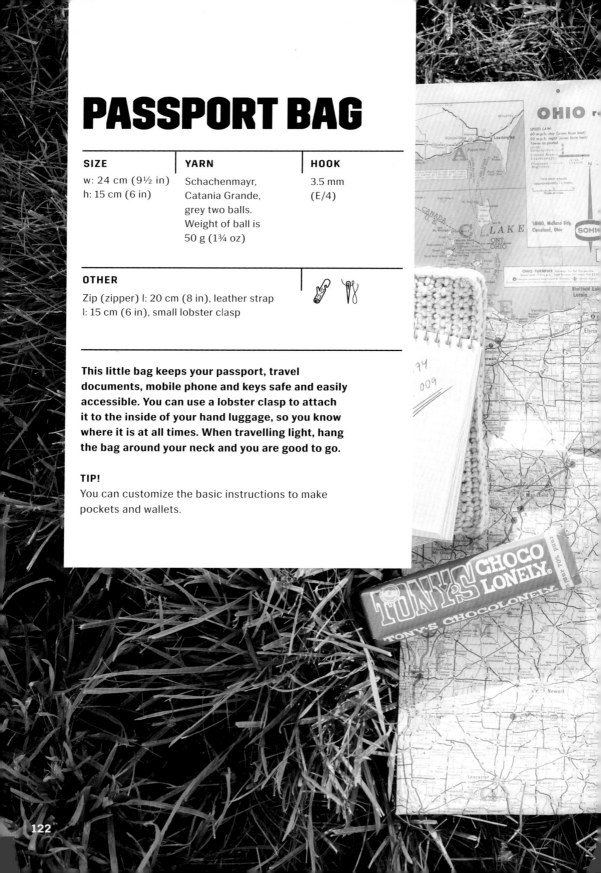

This little bag keeps your passport, travel documents, mobile phone and keys safe and easily accessible. You can use a lobster clasp to attach it to the inside of your hand luggage, so you know where it is at all times. When travelling light, hang the bag around your neck and you are good to go.

TIP!
You can customize the basic instructions to make pockets and wallets.

1. The make is worked back and forth using double (single) crochet stitches (see page 234 for step-by-step instructions). Chain 41 stitches to begin. Put the hook through the second stitch from the hook and crochet 39 dc (sc), then turn. Crochet 1 ch to begin the second row, then crochet 1 dc (sc) into each stitch, putting the hook through both loops of the stitch in the row below. Make sure the work does not increase or decrease at the edges while crocheting. The single chain stitch at the edges replaces the first double (single) crochet stitch. Now and again, check that each row contains 40 dc (sc). Crochet 30 rows in total, cut the yarn and fasten off. Repeat to crochet a second piece.

2. Sew one side of the zip (zipper) to one crochet piece, one row from the top edge.

3. Sew the other side of the zip (zipper) to the other crochet piece.

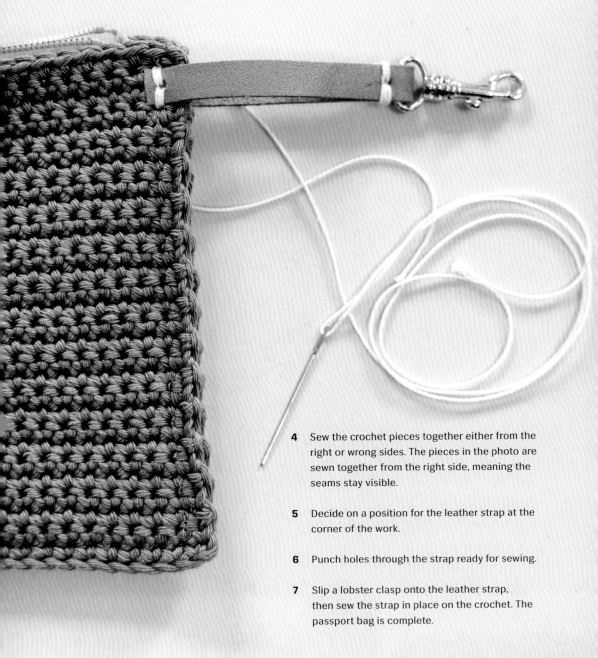

4 Sew the crochet pieces together either from the right or wrong sides. The pieces in the photo are sewn together from the right side, meaning the seams stay visible.

5 Decide on a position for the leather strap at the corner of the work.

6 Punch holes through the strap ready for sewing.

7 Slip a lobster clasp onto the leather strap, then sew the strap in place on the crochet. The passport bag is complete.

USING THE SAME TECHNIQUE, YOU CAN MAKE
different types of pockets and bags. The small
grey pocket is made using Catania Grande yarn.
It is 26 double (single) crochet stitches wide and
21 rows high. A 50-g (1¾-oz) ball of yarn is enough
to make the pocket.

The striped wallet is crocheted using a mid-thick
Catania yarn. Half a ball per colour is sufficient. The
make is 35 chain stitches wide and 106 rows high,
using a 2.0 mm (B/1) hook. The stripes are two rows
thick. Fold the work in half and sew a zip (zipper) in
place at the mouth of the second pocket.

BIKE BAG

SIZE	YARN	HOOK
w: 20 cm (8 in) h: 16 cm (6¼ in)	Hilos, La Espiga, grey approx. 150 g (5 oz)	2.5 mm (B/1)

OTHER	
Zip (zipper) l: 18 cm (7 in), two leather belts l: 50cm (19¾ in) each	

This is a brilliant little bike bag that could also be attached to your belt. Made using Mexican nylon yarn, the crocheted bag won't lose its shape, and will dry in a jiffy if you get caught in a shower. Here the leather straps are used to fix the bag over the handlebars, but you could also fasten it under the crossbar.

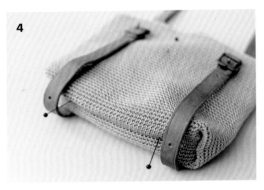

1   Pin the zip (zipper) one row from the top edge on each side and sew in place. A zip (zipper) that opens all the way is easier to work with.

2   Sew the bottom seam closed, one stitch at a time.

3   On the inside, sew across the corners at both ends of the bottom seam. Fasten the resulting triangular points to the wrong side of the work with a few sturdy stitches.

The bag is worked in a tube using double (single) crochet stitches (see page 236 for step-by-step instructions).

   Chain 115 stitches to begin and close into a ring with a slip stitch. Crochet 1 dc (sc) into each chain stitch. Move seamlessly to the next round in a spiral. Continue crocheting 1 dc (sc) into each stitch, putting the hook through both loops of the stitch in the row below. The work consists of 50 rounds. Finish the upper edge with a round of ss.

4   Decide where you want the leather straps to be positioned on the bag. Here they are about 8 cm (3¼ in) apart. Allow about 10 cm (4 in) of space between the top of the bag and the bend in the straps for hanging the bag on the bike.

5   Punch holes in the leather in line with the top front, the bottom and the back top of each strap, and use strong sewing thread to sew the straps in place.

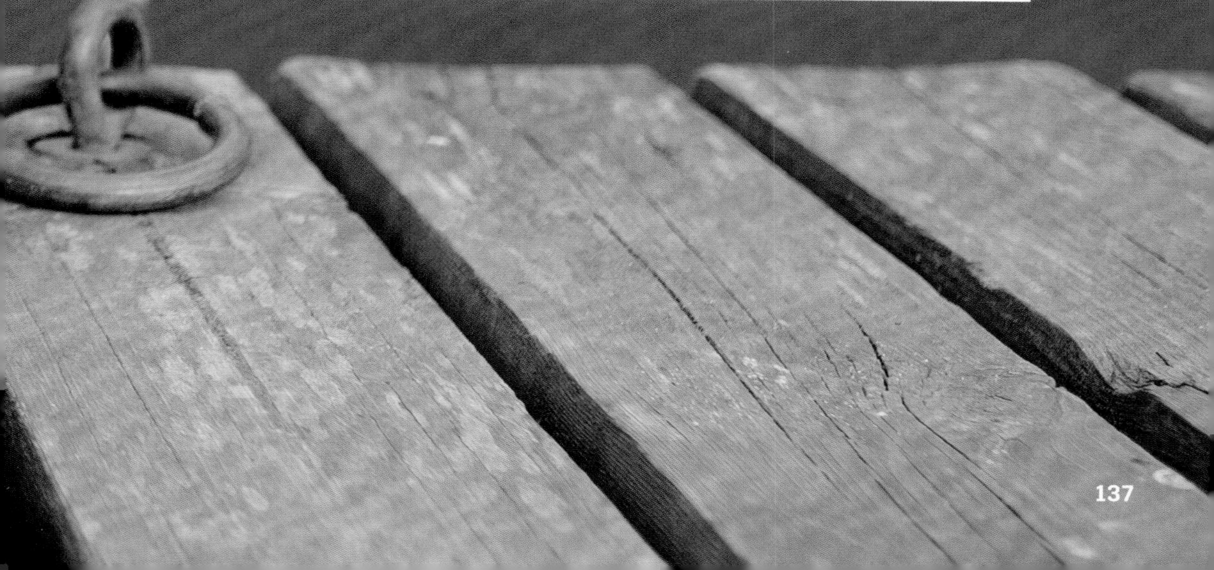

TOILETRY BAG

SIZE	YARN	HOOK
w: 32 cm (12⅝ in) h: 32 cm (12⅝ in) base d: 12 cm (5 in)	Liina fish net twine, 12-ply, off-white approx. 120 g (4 oz), black approx. 80g (2¾ oz)	1.75 mm (size 6)

OTHER	
Waterproof lining fabric 40 x 35 cm (15¾ x 13¾ in), zip (zipper) l: 30 cm (12 in), leather belt l: 75 cm (29½ in)	

A toiletry bag is a small but necessary travel essential that ensures you don't arrive at your destination with shampoo-coated socks or a large stain inside your suitcase. However, it is not until the time comes to pack for your next trip that you once again realize that a toiletry bag has been on your shopping list for the past two years. Cross that entry off the list by crocheting this brick-patterned, plastic-lined toiletry bag.

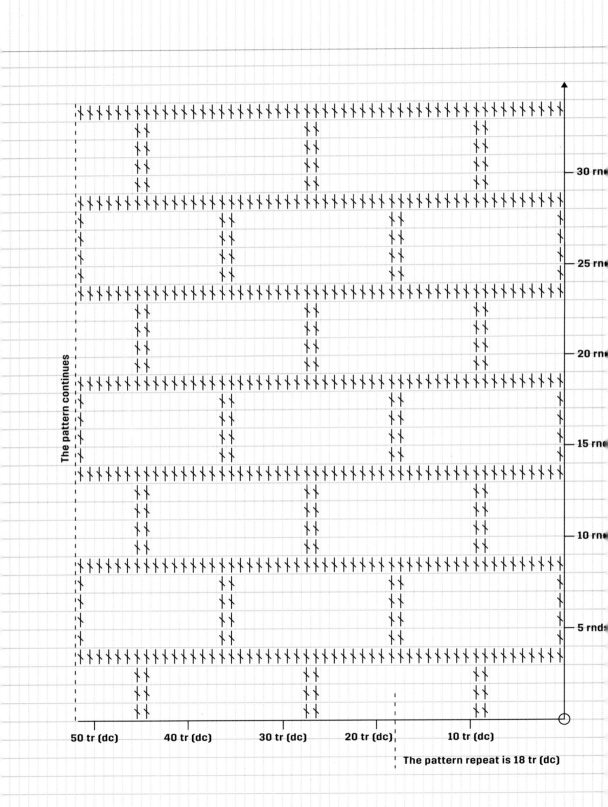

The pattern continues

30 rnd

25 rnd

20 rnd

15 rnd

10 rnd

5 rnds

50 tr (dc)   40 tr (dc)   30 tr (dc)   20 tr (dc)   10 tr (dc)

The pattern repeat is 18 tr (dc)

CROCHET INSTRUCTIONS

The make is worked in a tube using a two-colour pillar technique (see page 246 for step-by-step instructions). The non-working yarn is carried along within the pillars while working.

Rnd 1. Chain 180 stitches with the off-white yarn to begin, chaining loose stitches so they won't strain in the final make. Check that your work isn't twisted, then close it into a ring using a slip stitch. Ch 3 stitches with the off-white yarn to form the first pillar of the round. Carry the black yarn. Work 6 treble (double) crochet stitches with the off-white yarn, change to the black yarn on the last yarn over hook of the next pillar. Crochet 1 tr (dc) with the black yarn, then change back to the off-white yarn on the last yoh of the next pillar. The pattern repeat consists of 16 tr (dc) with the off-white yarn and 2 tr (dc) with the black. Close the round with a ss into the third stitch from the start.

Rnds 2–3. Work as for rnd 1. At the end of the third round, make the slip stitch's yarn over hook with the black yarn so that the fourth round begins with black.

Rnd 4. Crochet a tr(dc)-round wholly with the black yarn. Carry the off-white yarn along within the pillars. Close the round with a ss.

Rnd 5. Ch 3 stitches with the black yarn, then change to the off-white yarn. Crochet 15 tr (dc) with the off-white yarn, then change to black on the last yoh of the next pillar. Crochet 1 tr (dc) with black, then change back to the off-white yarn on the last yoh of the next pillar. The pattern repeat consists of 16 tr (dc) with the off-white yarn and 2 tr (dc) with black.

Continue following the chart. The work consists of 54 rounds in total, and the last round is crocheted wholly in black. Carry the non-working yarn to the end of the work. Finish the upper edge with a round of ss. Cut the yarn and fasten off.

pillar, black

pillar, off-white

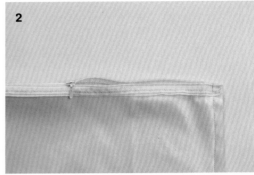

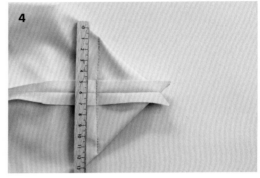

SEWING

1 Cut two identical pieces of lining fabric, taking your measurements from the size of the crochet bag, and adding 2 cm (¾ in) seam allowances to the height and length. Sew the zip (zipper) to the upper edges of the lining pieces, making sure that the right side of the zip (zipper) and the seam allowance end up on the same side of the lining.

2 Sew the remaining three edges together.

3 Sew the crochet bag's bottom edge closed by hand, one stitch at a time.

4 Measure a line 12 cm (4¾ in) long across each corner of the lining seam and sew across with sturdy stitches.

5 Repeat Step 4 at the bottom of the crochet bag.

6 Wrap the leather belt around the middle of the bag, with the buckle about 20 cm (8 in) up from the bag's bottom seam.

7 Punch holes in the belt in three places: one hole at the front, below the clasp; one in line with the bag's seam; and two at the back. Use strong thread to sew the belt to the bag through the holes.

8 Wrong sides together and matching the top edges, put the lining inside the crochet bag. Along the edges of the zip (zipper), sew the lining to the bag by hand using small stitches.

9 The toiletry bag is complete.

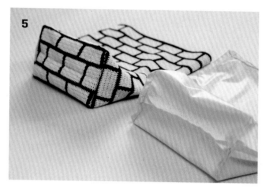

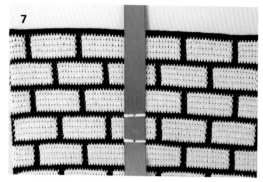

ANCHOR BAG

SIZE	YARN	HOOK
w: 40 cm (15¾ in) h: 47 cm (18½ in)	Lamana, Ica, red two balls. Weight of ball is 50 g (1¾ oz)	3.5 mm (E/4)

OTHER	
Grey cotton fabric 2 x 50 x 45 cm (19¾ x 17¾ in), cotton lining fabric, 2 x 50 x 45 cm (19¾ x 17¾ in), textile glue, strong cotton webbing for straps 2 x 75 cm (29½ in)	

The stormy sea is symbolic of life's ups and downs, so the anchor motif depicted on this sturdy bag denotes strength, determination and the ability to weather storms. This bag's shoulder straps are also strong and won't break in a hurry. The yarn chosen for the crochet in this project is ordinarily used for finishing carpet edges, so again, strength is a common theme.

CROCHET INSTRUCTIONS

The anchor is crocheted in four pieces: a column; a smaller horizontal line; the lower curve; and a circle. The pieces are crocheted in half-pillars, and shaped by adding stitches. A half-pillar is worked in the same way as the beginning of a pillar, so catch the yarn over hook, put the hook through the next stitch, yoh, then pull through to the right side of the work. There are now three stitches on the hook. Make a new yoh and pull through all the stitches on the hook. A half-pillar is the intermediate form of a pillar and a double (single) crochet stitch.

1. HORIZONTAL LINE

Row 1. Chain 19 stitches to begin. Crochet a half-pillar on the third stitch from the hook. The chain stitches in the beginning count as the first half-pillar. Continue the row by crocheting a half-pillar into each stitch.

Row 2. Ch 2 stitches, then crochet a half-pillar into each of the half-pillars in the previous row, putting the hook through both loops of the stitch.

Row 3. Crochet as for the previous row.

Row 4. Crochet a round of dc (sc) stitches right around the edge, working 1 dc (sc) into each half-pillar and 6 dc (sc) on the short sides, that is 2 dc (sc) into each beginning of each row. Cut the yarns and weave in ends.

2. COLUMN

Crochet as for the horizontal line, but ch 36 stitches to begin.

3. CURVE

Row 1. Ch 51 stitches to begin. Crochet a half-pillar into the third stitch from the beginning. The chain stitches in the beginning count as the first half-pillar. Continue the row by crocheting two half-pillars into every fifth stitch; crochet one half-pillar into each of the intervening stitches. At the end of the row there are 60 half-pillars, and the work should curve outward a little.

Row 2. Ch 2 stitches, then crochet one half-pillar into each of the previous row's half-pillars.

Row 3. Work as for the previous row.

Row 4. Crochet a round of dc (sc) around the edge of the piece, as for the horizontal line. Cut the yarns and weave in ends.

4. CIRCLE

Rnd 1. Ch 28 stitches to begin, leaving a 100-cm (39-in) yarn end at the beginning. Make sure the work isn't twisted, then close it into a ring with a ss. Ch 2 stitches to form the first half-pillar. Continue by crocheting two half-pillars into every other chain stitch; crochet one half-pillar into each of the intervening stitches. Close the round with a slip stitch in the third chain stitch from the beginning. The round consists of 42 half-pillars in total.

Rnd 2. Ch 2 stitches, then crochet one half-pillar into each of the previous round's half-pillars. Close the round with a ss.

Rnd 3. Crochet 1 ch, then crochet a dc(sc)-round, working 1 dc (sc) into each half-pillar. Close the round with a ss. Use the yarn end at the beginning to crochet a dc(sc)-round around the inner rim, working 1 dc (sc) into each stitch. Cut the yarn and weave in the ends.

SEWING

1 Mark the central point on the front piece of cotton fabric, then lay the anchor pieces in place so that the anchor is about 10 cm (4 in) up from what will be the lower edge of the bag. Start by gluing the column in place, centred on the marked spot, using a little textile glue: the pieces will also be sewn on later. Next, glue on the anchor's circle and curve. Decide where you would like the horizontal line to sit, then glue in place.

2 Allow the glue to dry, then sew around the anchor pieces as a single shape, sewing along the edges.

3 Right sides together, sew around three sides of the cotton pieces to make a bag. Repeat with the lining fabric pieces.

4 Measure a line 10 cm (4 in) long across the two bottom corners of the bag and lining and sew across.

5 Cut away the surplus fabric from the corners. Turn under and sew a narrow hem around the top edges of the bag and lining. Wrong sides together, put the lining inside the bag, matching the side seams, and sew around the top edge.

6 The bag is ready to have straps attached.

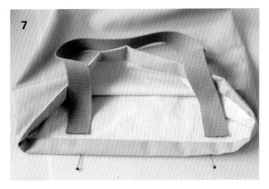

7 Turn under a 3-cm (1¼-in) hem around the top edge and iron smooth. Tuck the strap ends under the hem, about 10 cm (4 in) in from the sides of the bag.

8 Sew around the hem, sewing over the ends of the straps.

9 The straps are sewn on.

10 Fold the straps up, and on the right side of the bag sew them in place with a line of stitches. The anchor bag is complete.

CAN CARRIER

SIZE	YARN	HOOK
To carry four 330-ml (11-fl oz) cans	Lamana, Ica, four balls. Weight of ball is 50 g (1¾ oz)	3.5 mm (E/4)

OTHER	
Two leather belts l: 40 cm (15¾ in) and 12 cm (5 in)	

For picnics, parties or nipping to the shop, this can carrier is way cooler than a plastic bag. You'll certainly stand out from the crowd with this accessory, which doesn't have to be used for cans. Your craftsmanship will be clear to all, and you'll soon find yourself exchanging handicraft tips and phone numbers with new acquaintances.

1 **Rnd 1.** Wrap yarn around your finger twice and work 20 double (single) crochet stitches into the loop. Crochet in the yarn end along with a few of the stitches and pull on it at the end of the round if the foundation chain is too loose.

2 **Rnd 2.** Move seamlessly to the next round in a spiral. Put the hook through both loops of the stitch in the row below, then crochet 1 dc (sc) into each stitch. The round contains 20 dc (sc) in total.

Rnd 3. Crochet 2 dc (sc) into every second stitch; crochet 1 dc (sc) into each of the intervening stitches. The round contains 30 dc (sc) in total.

Rnd 4. Crochet a dc(sc)-round without increases.

Rnd 5. Crochet 2 dc (sc) into every third stitch; crochet 1 dc (sc) into each of the intervening stitches. The round contains 40 dc (sc) in total.

7

3 **Rnds 6–22.** Crochet dc(sc)-rounds. If the work is too snug or too loose for the cans, unravel back to rnd 5 and either add on an increase round, or unravel further to rnd 4. Your choice of yarn and personal crochet tension will influence the final size.

4 **Rnd 23.** The belt loop is crocheted during this round. Chain 3 stitches, then miss (skip) three stitches and attach the ch-arch to the fourth stitch with a dc (sc) stitch. Continue by crocheting 1 dc (sc) into each stitch.

5 **Rnd 24.** Crochet a dc(sc)-round, working 1 dc (sc) into each stitch. At the belt loop, crochet 3 dc (sc) into the ch-arch of the previous round.
Rnd 25. Crochet a dc(sc)-round.

6 Finish the upper edge with a round of slip stitches. Cut the yarn and fasten off.

7 Crochet another three identical can carriers. You'll need two belts that are narrow enough to slip through the belt loops, one cut to 12 cm (5 in) long and the other to 40 cm (15¾ in) long.

8

9

10

11

8 Punch a hole through the shorter belt, 8 cm (3¼ in) from the buckle, and slip it through the belt loops of two of the can carriers.

9 Thread the second belt through the two other can carriers.

10 Position the shorter belt over the longer belt to bring the four carriers together.

11 The can carrier is complete, and you can safely transport upright cans by hand, or over the handlebars of your bike.

JAAKKO, WHO RUNS THE LEGENDARY KÄPYLÄN KISKA in Helsinki, pours me a latte with attitude. The café was opened by a couple of world travellers who wanted to create an open-minded community where everyone is welcome, and where living art is readily available. In the summer, flea markets pop up in the café gardens, where live music is played and a handwritten sign directs you to the best organic ice cream.

FOLK BAG

SIZE	YARN	HOOK
w: 48 cm (19 in)	Liina fish net twine, 18-ply,	2.25 mm
h: 55 cm (21½ in)	off-white approx. 400 g	(B/1)
crochet h: 47 cm	(14 oz), black approx.	
(18½ in)	200 g (7 oz)	

OTHER

Cotton fabric for the inner pocket,
strong cotton webbing for the
straps 2 x 85 cm (34 in), thick
cotton cords for the insides of
the straps, leather for the base

Toomas carries a maxi-bag patterned with
traditional Finnish landscape motifs, such as bears,
cows and elks. Alpacas have also made it into the
mix. There are a few alpaca farms in Finland where
you can make the acquaintance of these mild and
quiet South American animals, and alpaca wool is a
great choice when crocheting winter clothes.

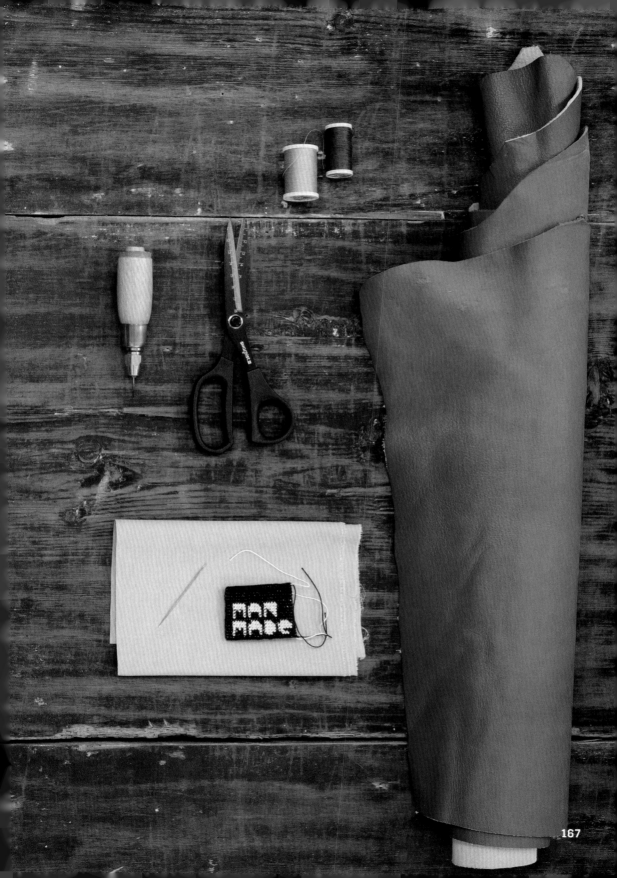

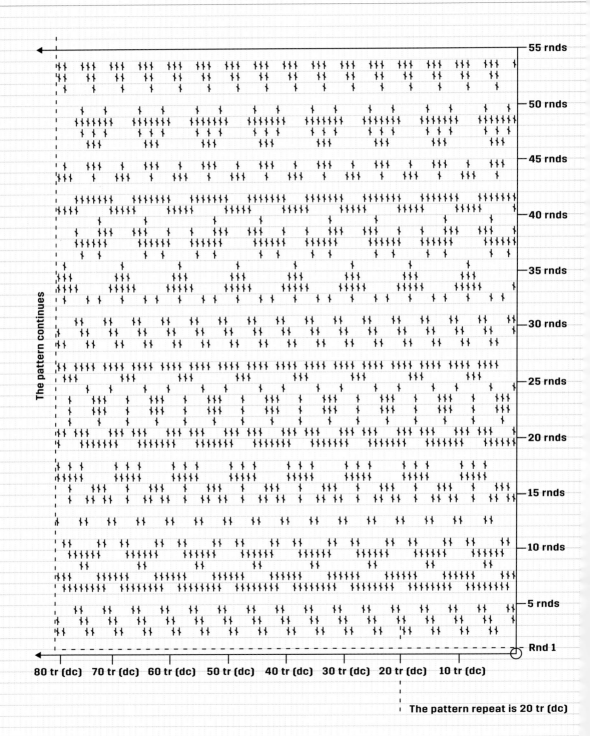

The pattern continues

55 rnds

50 rnds

45 rnds

40 rnds

35 rnds

30 rnds

25 rnds

20 rnds

15 rnds

10 rnds

5 rnds

Rnd 1

80 tr (dc)   70 tr (dc)   60 tr (dc)   50 tr (dc)   40 tr (dc)   30 tr (dc)   20 tr (dc)   10 tr (dc)

The pattern repeat is 20 tr (dc)

CROCHET INSTRUCTIONS

The make is worked as a tube using a two-colour pillar technique (see page 246 for step-by-step instructions). The non-working yarn is carried along within the pillars while working.

Rnd 1. Chain 220 stitches with the off-white yarn to begin, chaining loose stitches so they won't strain in the final make. Check that your work isn't twisted, then close it into a ring using a slip stitch. Crochet the first round with double (single) crochet stitches using the off-white yarn, working 1 dc (sc) into every chain stitch. Carry the black yarn. The dc(sc)-round will be the bag's bottom seam allowance. Close the round with a ss into the first chain stitch.

Rnd 2. Ch 3 stitches with the off-white yarn to form the first pillar of the round. Carry the black yarn. Crochet a round of treble (double) crochet stitches with the off-white yarn, working 1 tr (dc) into each chain stitch. Close the round with a ss into the third chain stitch from the beginning.

Rnd 3. Ch 3 stitches with the off-white yarn to begin. Carry the black yarn, crochet 1 tr (dc) with the off-white yarn, then change to the black yarn on the last yarn over hook of the next pillar. Crochet 1 tr (dc) with the black yarn, then change back to the off-white yarn in the next pillar. The pattern repeat for this round consists of 3 tr (dc) with the off-white yarn, and 2 tr (dc) with the black yarn. Close the round with a ss, making the yoh with the black yarn.

Rnd 4. Ch 3 stitches with the black yarn, then change to the off-white yarn. Crochet 2 tr (dc), then change to the black yarn on the last yoh of the third pillar. Continue working the round, following the chart. Close the round with a ss.

Continue working, following the chart. The work consists of 55 rounds in total, of which the last is crocheted wholly with the off-white yarn. Carry the black yarn to the end of the work. Crochet a dc(sc)-round with the off-white yarn to strengthen the upper edge, and finish with a round of ss. Cut the yarns and fasten off.

pillar, black

pillar, off-white

TO MAKE A POCKET, cut two pieces of cotton, each 20 x 30 cm (8 x 12 in). At the top of one piece hem 2 cm (¾ in), then repeat. Place it on top of the other pocket piece, right sides facing. Sew three edges together and turn the work right sides out. Press the seams and sew another two 1 cm (⅜ in) hems on the long edges to the right side of the pocket. Fold a 2 cm (¾ in) turn to the wrong side of the upper edge of the pocket. Position the pocket centred along the top edge of the bag. Fold over the ends of the straps by 5cm (2in).

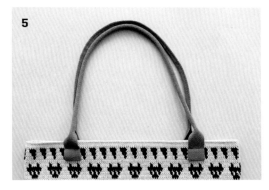

SEWING

1. Sew the pocket in position along the top edge of the bag.

2. Position each folded strap end a few rounds down from the top of the bag on the right side of the crochet, 10 cm (4 in) from the sides of the bag, and pin in place. Open out the folds in the straps and sew along the creases with sturdy stitches. Then flip the straps upwards and stitch them on the right side as well.

3. Fold the straps in half lengthwise, and sew the edges together. Leave a 3-cm (1¼-in) gap at both ends of the straps for threading the cotton cords through.

4. Thread a cotton cord through each strap, then cut the ends of the cords so they aren't visible. The cords make the straps sturdier.

5. The straps are complete.

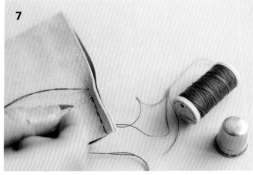

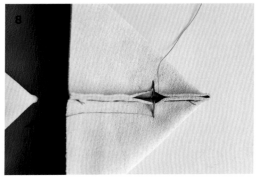

6 Cut the leather piece to measure 24 cm (9½ in) by the width of the bag plus 2 cm (¾ in) seam allowance. There will not be a bottom seam.

7 Fold the piece in half lengthwise, and sew the short sides closed, taking a 1 cm (⅜ in) seam allowance at each end. Use a leather needle and strong thread and sew the seams by hand.

8 Fold the bottom corners of the leather piece into triangles, then measure a line 5 cm (2 in) long across the seam. Sew along the line with sturdy stitches.

9 Right sides together and sewing by hand, stitch the leather piece to the dc(sc)-round at the bottom of the crochet. You can also use a sewing awl for the leather seams (see page 12). When using the awl, use the sturdiest thread possible.

10 The folk bag is complete.

LUMBERJACK'S BACKPACK

SIZE	YARN	HOOK
w: 42 cm (16½ in) h: 60 cm (23⅝ in) crochet h: 34 cm (13⅜ in) base d: 12 cm (5 in)	Schachenmayr, Catania Grande, red five balls, black five balls. Weight of ball is 50 g (1¾ oz)	3.5 mm (E/4)

OTHER

Sturdy cotton fabric for the top and bottom of the bag and the lining l: 90 cm (35½ in), w: 150 cm (60 in), wadding, leather straps 2 x 75 cm (29½ in), four flat rivets for fastening the straps, two metal rings d: 2.5 cm (1 in), one metal ring d: 5 cm (2 in), leather cord l: 120 cm (47¼ in)

A properly designed backpack supports your posture and lightens even the heaviest loads. This chequered lumberjack's backpack is as suitable for the city streets as it is for rugged trails: in the photo, Mickaël carries his backpack through Haaga's rhododendron park. You can crochet yours in this timeless red and black check, or shake it up a bit with lighter, summery colours.

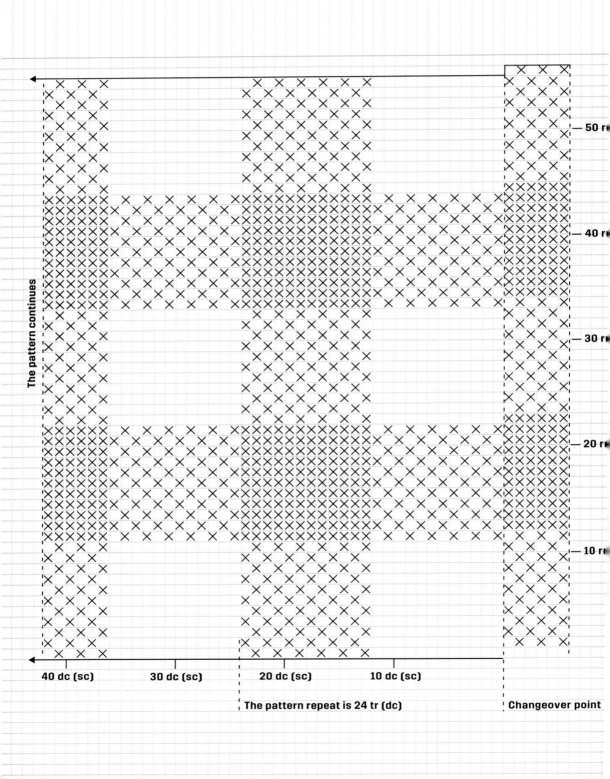

The pattern continues

— 50 r
— 40 r
— 30 r
— 20 r
— 10 r

40 dc (sc)　　　30 dc (sc)　　　20 dc (sc)　　　10 dc (sc)

The pattern repeat is 24 tr (dc)　　　　Changeover point

CROCHET INSTRUCTIONS

Double (single) crochet stitches are worked in a tube using the optical crochet technique. This technique is otherwise the same as for double (single) crochet (see page 236 for step-by-step instructions), but, starting from the second row, put the hook through only the front loop of the stitch in the row below. This small change makes vertical lines possible, so you can crochet vertical patterns in a tube. The non-working yarn is carried along the stitches throughout.

Rnd 1. Chain 168 stitches with the red yarn to begin. Check that your work isn't twisted and close it into a ring with a slip stitch. Carry the black yarn; it is crocheted within the dc (sc) stitches. Crochet 10 dc (sc) with the red yarn, then change to the black yarn on the last yarn over hook of the next stitch. Crochet the next 12 dc (sc) by alternating between the red and black yarns on every stitch: the colour change always happens by making the last yarn over hook of a stitch with a new colour. You can find the instructions for changing colours on page 242. Next, crochet 12 dc (sc) with the red yarn, and the following 12 by alternating between black and red. Repeat to the end of the round; the round's last stitch is red. Move seamlessly to the next round in a spiral.

Rnd 2. The optical crochet begins on this round. In the following rounds you'll put the hook through only the front loop of the stitch in the row below, while the non-working yarn is carried along within the stitches throughout. Crochet 12 dc (sc) with red to begin, and the next 12 dc (sc) by alternating between red and black. On this round, crochet 1 red dc (sc) into the previous round's black dc (sc), and vice versa. Use the chart to check stitch colours and crochet to the end of the round.

Rnds 3–11. Crochet the rounds, following the chart, while carrying the non-working yarn.

Rnd 12. On this round, crochet black and red squares into the previous round's red squares, and black squares into the previous round's black and red squares.

Continue crocheting, following the chart. Remember to only put the hook through the front loop of the stitch, and to carry the non-working yarn along within the stitches throughout.

A small pattern change will form at the round's changeover point: see the chart. The lumberjack's backpack consists of 55 rounds in total, that is five checks. Cut the yarns and fasten off.

☐ double (single) crochet stitch, red

☒ double (single) crochet stitch, black

SEWING

1   Cut pieces of cotton fabric for the top and bottom pieces of the make and the lining. For the bottom cut a piece 88 x 20 cm (34$^5/_8$ x 8 in). Cut the same size piece from the wadding. For the top cut a piece of cotton 88 x 65 cm (34$^5/_8$ x 25$^5/_8$ in). Measure the crochet and cut two pieces of cotton fabric to make a lining bag. Sew the three seams of the lining bag closed. Cut a strip of cotton fabric 12 x 50 cm (4$^3/_4$ x 19$^3/_4$ in) to use for the metal-ring fastening. Fold it in half lengthwise, press and fold again to make it hardwearing.

2   Fold the upper and lower pieces in half with the right sides facing. Mark the halfway point on the other edge with a pin, and sew the other edge closed on both pieces. Sew the wadding along with the lower piece. Sew the wadding and lower edge to the crochet, one dc(sc)-round from the edge. Leave a 1.5-cm ($^5/_8$-in) seam allowance to the lower piece.

3   Sew the fastening strips closed, close to the edge. The final width of the fastening strip is 3 cm (1$^1/_4$ in).

4 Mark the positions for the fastening strips on the lower piece of fabric, 7 cm (2¾ in) from the edges. Thread the strips through the metal rings, then pin the strips to the edges of the lower piece. Fasten the ends of the strips next to each other as shown in the photo, so that your sewing machine needle doesn't snap sewing areas that are too thick. Mark a space for the large metal ring's fastening strap at the middle of the upper edge of the crochet.

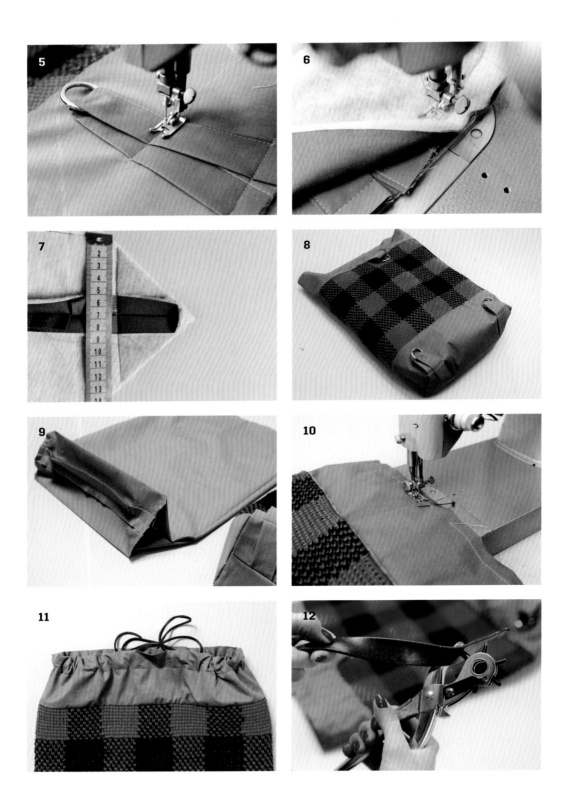

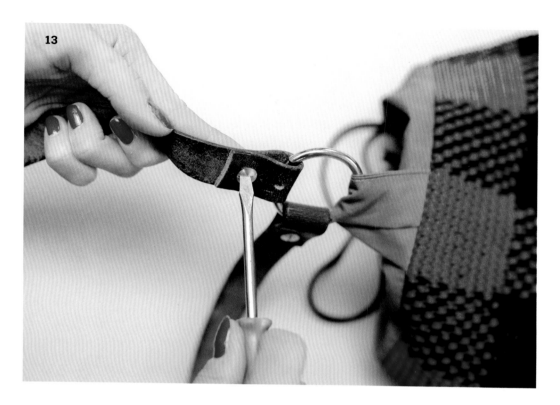

5 Sew the fastening straps securely onto the places marked at the upper and lower borders. Sew the strips on the lower edge in two places; the upper row of stitches is 8 cm (3¼ in) from the upper edge.

6 Sew the bottom edge seam closed.

7 Turn the work wrong side out and open the corners and their seam allowances. Measure a line 12 cm (5 in) long across each corner of the seam.

8 Sew the triangular seams closed with several rows of sturdy stitches.

9 Sew corner seams in the lining bag .

10 Place the lining inside the cover, right sides facing. Sew the lining to the upper edge, leaving a 5-cm (2-in) gap to the front for threading cord through.

11 Turn the bag right side out and sew the turning gap closed. Place the lining inside the bag and run a line of stitches to make a cord passage 3 cm (1¼ in) from the edge. Thread the leather cord through.

12 Punch holes where you want to screw the flat rivets, or sew the straps. Measure the length of the straps to suit your own use; the straps in these instructions are 75 cm (29½ in) long.

13 Fasten the straps securely to the metal rings at the upper and lower borders. If using flat rivets, screw them tightly. If sewing the straps on, use strong thread.

THE MID-BACK STRAP FASTENING is sturdy and ergonomic, and stops the backpack sliding to one shoulder. Use cotton straps rather than leather ones if you want the backpack to be washable. Straps fastened with flat rivets can be removed for washing. The crochet might shrink a little in the wash, so be careful with the water temperature. The lumberjack backpack is best washed in a cool lake really.

EQUIPMENT

4

succaplokki
accessories
ДЕКСТРИН
Molla
KALALANKA
SUOMEN LANKA
WRITERSBLOK®
KRAFT
NOTES
BLOC DE NOTES
126 Ultra thin pages
Made with recycled paper
126 feuillets ultra fins
Fait de papier recyclé

YARN CHAIN

SIZE	YARN	HOOK
Variable	Schachenmayr, Catania Fine, grey approx. 50 g (1¾ oz)	1.5 mm (size 8)

OTHER	
Split ring	

This project allows you to crochet any number of chain links and join them together to make a key chain that is light but bulky, so you won't lose it. Chains are so versatile that if you get carried away crocheting the links, you're bound to come up with a use for them.

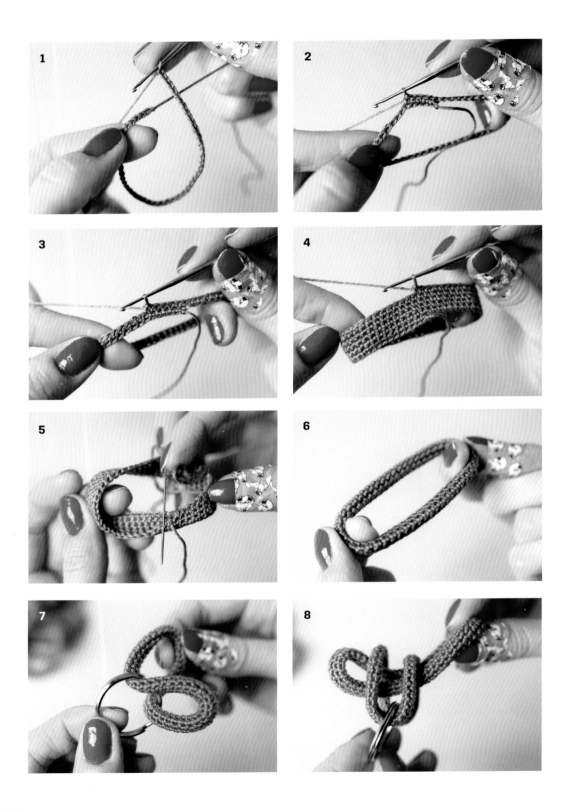

1 Chain 55 stitches to begin.

2 Make sure your work isn't twisted, then close it into a ring with a double (single) crochet stitch. Continue crocheting 1 dc (sc) into each stitch.

3 At the round's start point, move seamlessly to the next round in a spiral. See page 236 for step-by-step instructions for double (single) crochet stitching in the round.

4 Crochet five rounds in total for one link.

5 Cut the yarn, leaving a 30-cm (12-in) yarn end for the sewing. Fold the work in half with the right side out, and sew the upper and lower edges together, one stitch at a time.

6 Fasten off the yarns and weave in the ends. Roll the seam to the inside of the link. Crochet the desired amount of identical links; the key chain here consists of 13 links.

7 Thread the first crocheted link through the split ring.

8 Fold that link in half, then thread the second link through the first link.

9 Continue joining links in the same way. When the chain is the desired length, thread the ends of the final link onto the split ring.

UTILITY STRAP

SIZE	YARN	HOOK
l: 180 cm (70¼ in)	Climbing rope, thickness 3 mm (⅛ in), approx. 30 m (33 yd)	6.0 mm (J/10)

OTHER		
Two pieces of leather l: 9 cm (3½ in) each, textile glue		

A rope, a lasso, a leash; this make has many uses. Easily crochet the utility strap in your desired size and use it, for example, to carry your skateboard.

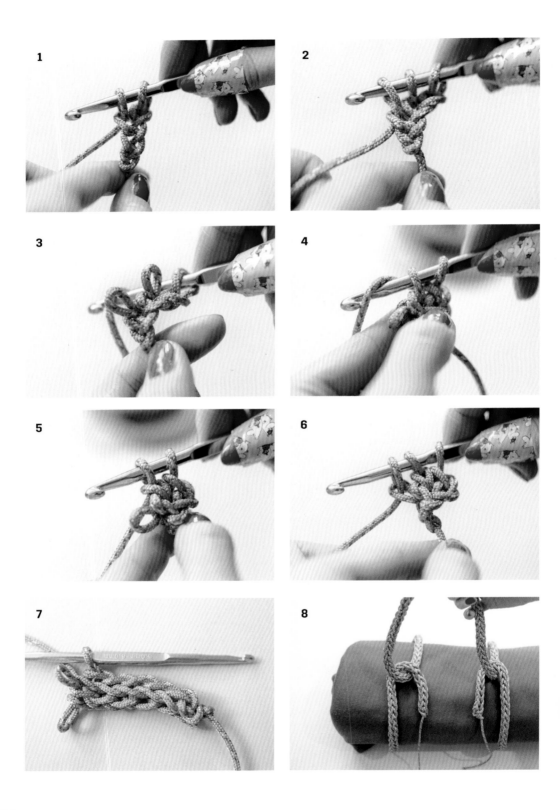

1 Make a slip knot on the hook, then chain 3 stitches.

2 Put the hook through the second stitch from the hook, yarn over hook and pull through to the right side of the work. There are now three stitches on the hook.

3 Drop two stitches from the hook, leaving one stitch. Yoh and ch 1 stitch into the stitch left on the hook. Keep a tight grip on your work to ensure the dropped stitches don't unravel.

4 Pull a yoh through the stitch on the hook. Catch the first dropped stitch on the hook and yoh.

5 Pull the yoh through the stitch on the hook. There are now two stitches on the hook.

6 Catch the second dropped stitch on the hook. Yoh and pull through the stitch on the hook. There are now three stitches on the hook.

7 Again, drop two stitches off the hook. Remember to keep a firm grip on your work. Catch one stitch on the hook and crochet 1 dc (sc). There are now two stitches on the hook. Catch the second stitch on the hook and crochet 1 dc (sc). There are now three stitches on the hook. Continue in the same way until the strap is the desired length.

8 Fold the ends of the strap into loops, making sure the strap itself runs through the loops.

9 Glue the ends of the strap closed as shown. Reinforce the glued fastening points with stitches made using strong thread.

10 Punch holes into small leather strips and use strong sewing thread to sew them over the glued ends of the loops.

11 The utility strap is complete.

FOOTBALL BAG

SIZE	YARN	HOOK
w: 60 cm (23⅝ in) l: 120 cm (47¼ in)	Liina fish net twine, 18-ply, grey approx. 300 g (10½ oz)	2.5 mm (B/1)

OTHER

Two cords for the straps
l: 120 cm (47¼ in) each,
drawstring for closing l: 130 cm
(51¼ in), quick-release lock

This ball bag is crocheted using fish net twine, so it is hardwearing and can stretch to the size of five footballs. In fact, it can be a useful carrier for any athlete. Throw in your skateboard, jump on your bike and let the summer begin.

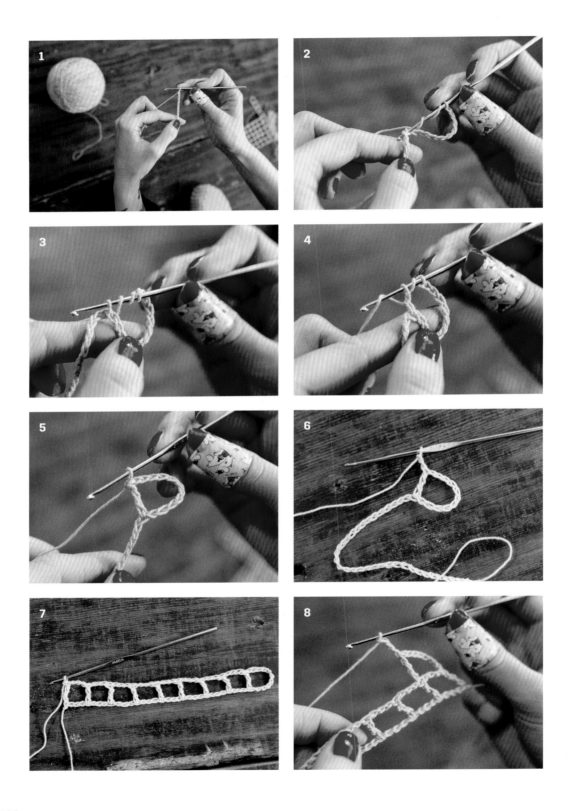

The photographs show the crochet steps in reduced size, whereas the text details the instructions for the actual football bag project. The bag is worked 40 squares wide, and 80 squares high. The work is crocheted using long pillars, made by catching the yarn over hook twice.

1   Chain 168 stitches to begin.

2   Long pillar: catch the yarn over hook twice, then put the hook through the twelfth chain stitch from the hook.

3   Yoh and pull through the stitch. There are now four stitches on the hook.

4   Yoh and pull through two of the stitches on the hook. Yoh again and pull through the next two stitches on the hook.

5   Yoh yet again, and pull through the last two stitches on the hook. One long pillar is now finished and the work contains the first finished square. The make is worked in the same way as the band poster on page 66, but the squares are larger.

6   Ch 3 stitches. In this make, three stitches are always chained in between each square.

7   Miss (skip) three stitches and crochet a long pillar into the fourth stitch. The work now contains its second square. Ch 3 stitches, again miss (skip) three stitches, then crochet a long pillar. Continue working in this way until there are 40 squares in the row. If your work contains too many stitches, open the slip knot and unravel the surplus stitches. The work won't unravel, because the chain stitches lock as they are worked. Leave one stitch for finishing. If your work contains too few stitches, you can chain extra stitches as needed with the yarn end.

8   Move to the next row by chaining 7 stitches to begin. Crochet a long pillar into the previous row's pillar. Ch 3 stitches and work another long pillar into the previous row's pillar.

9   Continue in the same way, with 7 ch to begin, a long pillar into the previous row's pillar, and always ch 3 stitches in between squares. Crochet 80 rows of squares.

10 Finish both short sides with a row of double (single) crochet. Crochet 3 dc (sc) into each square, and nothing into the pillars or along the long sides. Cut the yarn and fasten off.

FOLD THE FOOTBALL BAG IN HALF and weave the shoulder strap cords through the sides. Here, 6 mm (¼ in) strong climbing cord has been used. Weave the cord so that it runs through all the squares on each side to make the bag, adjust the length to suit the wearer, then cut the cord and tie a tight knot.

Weave a drawstring through the open upper edge, pull to close and fasten with a quick-release lock. The bag is ready for use.

SKATEBOARDER AND DRUMMER, NIKO, keeps his belongings safe in the ball bag while boarding on Suvilahti's skate ramp. He's been skateboarding for over ten years, and also performs in front of large crowds with his band. Skating is as consuming a hobby as crochet; once begun it becomes a way of life. However, with crochet you certainly get fewer bruises.

BUNTING

SIZE	YARN	HOOK
w: 25 cm (10 in)	Liina fish net twine,	1.75 mm
h: 30 cm (12 in)	18-ply, off-white	(size 6)
	approx. 80 g (2¾ oz)	

Yarn bombing as street art has quickly become a recognized form of urban decoration. Open-minded crafters are displaying their creations in new and surprising places all over town. Crochet-graffiti can be made with any type of yarn. Crochet your own bunting, tag it, then use it to bring colour and joy to your chosen location.

CROCHET INSTRUCTIONS

The make is worked back and forth using a pillar technique (see page 238 for step-by-step instructions).

Row 1. Chain 60 stitches to begin. Put the hook through the fourth stitch from the hook and crochet a pillar. Continue working 1 treble (double) crochet stitch into each stitch. The work is 58 tr (dc) wide.

Rows 2–24. Crochet tr(dc)-rows. Always ch 3 stitches at the beginning of each row to form the first pillar of the row. Continue crocheting 1 tr (dc) into each stitch in the row below, putting the hook through both loops.

Rows 25–the end. Decrease rows. Ch 2 stitches at the beginning of each row, and crochet 3 tr (dc) together at the end of each row. To do this, catch the yarn over hook, put the hook through both loops of the first pillar in the row below, yoh and pull through to the right side of the work. Repeat into the next two pillars. There are now four stitches on the hook. Yoh, and pull through all the stitches on the hook. One decrease is complete. Continue crocheting decrease rows until you only have a few pillars left in the row. Crochet the last pillars together, cut the yarn and fasten off. Crochet more bunting pieces in the same way.

Spray-paint your crochet or draw on it with fabric markers. To make a stencil, simply position masking tape or a cardboard mask over the work before you spray.

You can either sew a string along the top of the crochet pennants, or weave string through the pillars.

TRAVEL MIRROR

SIZE	YARN	HOOK
d: 13 cm (5¼ in)	Sirdar, Cotton DK, orange approx. 50 g (1¾ oz)	1.75 mm (size 6)

OTHER	
Mirror d: 12 cm (5 in), thick cardboard for mirror backing, tape, leather straps, two lobster clasps	

Whether on a fishing or a camping trip, this small mirror is the traveller's salvation, useful when you need to trim your beard or to send light signals to the neighbouring island. The crocheted casing features a place to keep your comb on the back, plus a hanging strap that means the mirror can be attached to your bag or hung up anywhere you can find a nail or a handy tree branch.

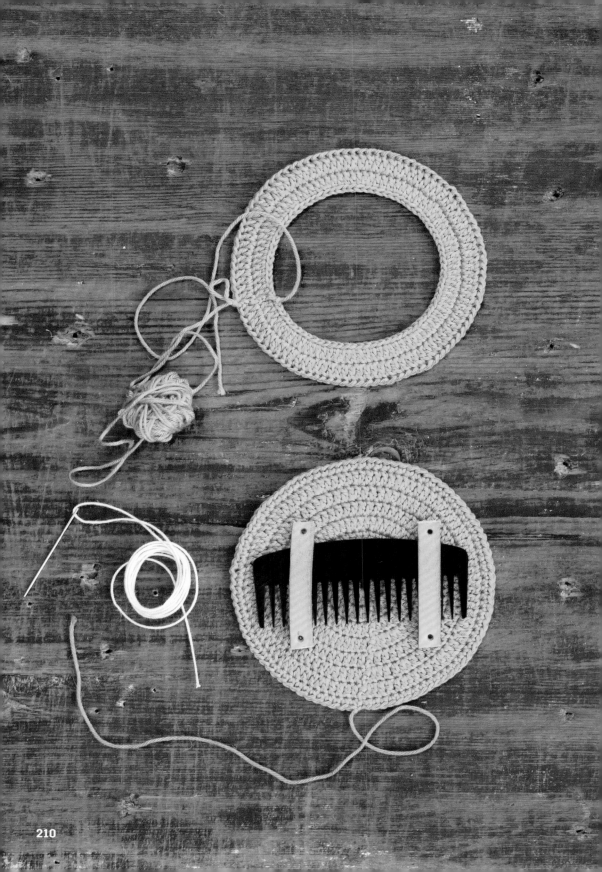

1

2

1 FRONT PIECE

Chain 80 stitches to begin. Make sure your work isn't twisted and close it into a ring with a slip stitch. Leave a 100-cm (39-in) yarn end to use for the inner edge's slip stitch round.

Rnd 1. Ch 3 stitches and work 1 treble (double) crochet stitch into the starting loop. Crochet 1 tr (dc) into the next four stitches, then crochet 2 tr (dc) into the next stitch. The round is worked by crocheting 2 tr (dc) into every fifth stitch, and 1 tr (dc) into each intervening stitch. Close the round with a ss into the third chain stitch from the beginning. The round consists of 96 tr (dc) in total.

Rnd 2. Crochet a tr(dc)-round without increasing. Don't cut the yarn, which will be used to crochet the pieces together. With the yarn end left at the start of the work, crochet a ss-round around the front piece's inner edge. Cut the yarn.

2 BACK PIECE

Rnd 1. Wrap yarn around a finger twice and hold the resulting loops between your thumb and index finger. Put the hook through the loops and pull a yarn over hook through. Your work now has one chain. Ch another 2 stitches to form the first pillar of the round. Crochet another 15 tr (dc) into the loop. Close the round with a ss into the third chain stitch from the beginning.

Rnd 2. Ch 3 to form the first pillar of each round. Crochet 1 tr (dc) into the starting loop. Putting the hook through both loops of the stitch in the row below, crochet 2 tr (dc) into each stitch. Close the round with a slip stitch into the third chain stitch from the beginning. The round consists of 32 tr (dc) in total.

Rnd 3. Ch 3 stitches and crochet 1 tr (dc) into the starting loop. In this round, crochet 2 tr (dc) into every other stitch and 1 tr (dc) into all intervening stitches. The round consists of 48 tr (dc) in total.

Rnd 4. Ch 3 stitches and crochet 1 tr (dc) into the starting loop. In this round, crochet 2 tr (dc) into every third stitch and 1 tr (dc) into all intervening stitches. The round consists of 64 tr (dc) in total.

Rnd 5. Crochet this round without increases, working 1 tr (dc) into each stitch.

Rnd 6. Ch 3 stitches and crochet 1 tr (dc) into the starting loop. Crochet 2 tr (dc) into every fourth stitch and 1 tr (dc) into all intervening stitches. The round consists of 80 tr (dc) in total.

Rnd 7. Ch 3 stitches and crochet 1 tr (dc) into the starting loop. Crochet 2 tr (dc) into every fifth stitch, and crochet 1 tr (dc) into all intervening stitches. The round consists of 96 tr (dc) in total.

Rnd 8. Crochet a dc(sc)-round, working 1 dc (sc) into each stitch. Cut the yarn.

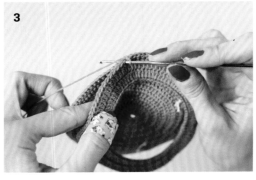

1   Cut the cardboard to the shape of the mirror, then attach it to the back of the mirror using tape around the edge.

2   Sew two short leather straps to the right side of the middle of the crocheted back piece.

3   Lay the back piece against the front piece with the wrong sides facing each other. Slip stitch the pieces together, one stitch at a time, to the halfway point.

4   Slide the mirror in between the crochet pieces. If it doesn't fit, add more rounds of crochet. If there is space left around the edges of the mirror, decrease the number of rounds.

5   Finish the edges with a round of ss. Cut the yarn and fasten off.

6   Tie the ends of the leather strap to the lobster clasps and slip the clasps through the stitches of the dc(sc)-round.

MAT BAG

SIZE	YARN	HOOK
l: 60 cm (23⅝ in) d: 14 cm (5½ in)	Liina fish net twine, 12-ply, black 150 g (5 oz), off-white 150 g (5 oz)	1.75 mm (size 6)

OTHER

Cotton fabric l: 20 cm (8 in)
w: 150 cm (60 in), cotton cord
for the straps l: 150 cm (60 in),
leather strip l: 30 cm (12 in)

Second only to crochet, yoga is one of my favourite pastimes. Everyone can benefit from the effects that regular practice has on posture, and from the way yoga clears the path to a stress-free mind. You can encourage that positive mind-body balance by crocheting a bag for your yoga mat.

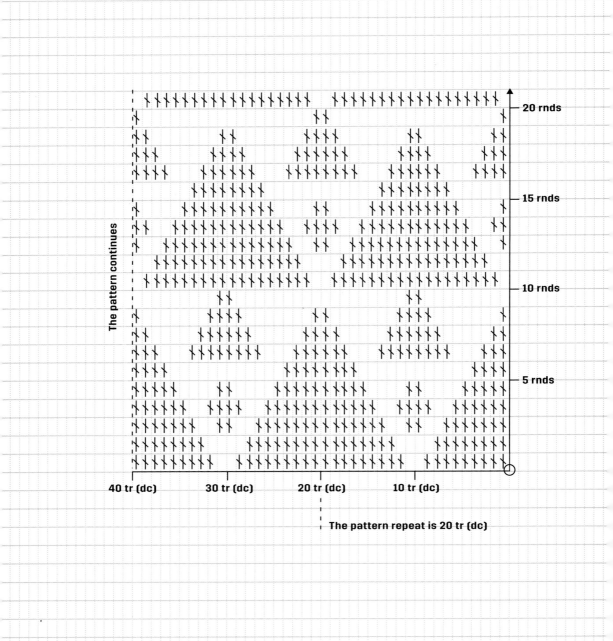

20 rnds

15 rnds

10 rnds

5 rnds

The pattern continues

40 tr (dc)　　　30 tr (dc)　　　20 tr (dc)　　　10 tr (dc)

The pattern repeat is 20 tr (dc)

CROCHET INSTRUCTIONS

The make is worked in a tube using a two-colour pillar technique (see page 246 for step-by-step instructions). Carry the non-working yarn along within the pillars throughout.

Rnd 1. Chain 120 stitches with the black yarn to begin, chaining loose stitches so they won't strain in the final make. Check that your work isn't twisted, then close it into a ring using a slip stitch. Ch 3 stitches with the black yarn to form the first pillar of the round. Carry the off-white yarn along. Work 7 treble (double) crochet stitches with the black yarn, then change to off-white on the last yarn over hook of the next pillar. Crochet 1 tr (dc) then change back to the black yarn on the last yoh of the next pillar. Crochet 9 tr (dc) to complete the repeat, which consists of 20 stitches. Close the round with a ss into the third chain stitch from the start.

Rnd 2. Ch 3 stitches, these always form the first pillar of each round. Crochet 6 tr (dc) with the black yarn, then change to the off-white yarn on the last yoh of the next pillar. Crochet 3 tr (dc) off-white then change back to the black yarn on the last yoh of the next pillar. Crochet 8 tr (dc) to complete the repeat, which consists of 20 stitches. Close the round with a ss.

Continue working, following the chart. The work contains 81 rounds in total, of which the last is worked entirely in off-white. Carry the non-working yarn along to the end. Crochet a dc(sc)-round along the upper edge, then finish with a ss-round. Cut the yarn and fasten off.

pillar, black

pillar, off-white

2 Fold the piece in half widthwise and right side out, and use zigzag stitch to sew the long edges together. Sew the two round bottom pieces together around the edges, again using zigzag stitch.

3 Turn the crochet tube inside out. Pin the bottom piece to one end of it and sew it in place, taking a 1 cm (³⁄₈ in) seam allowance.

4 Turn the bag right side out.

5 Sew the zigzagged edge of the strip to the open end of the crochet tube, one round from the edge. Leave a small gap in the middle of the upper edge for the strap.

Cut a circle of cotton fabric for the bottom of the bag to match the dimensions of the crochet, here 14 cm (5½ in) in diameter with 1 cm (³⁄₈ in) seam allowance all around. Cut a second identical circle. Cut a strip of cotton for the top of the bag, 16 cm (6¼ in) high, by the circumference of the crochet tube long.

1 Fold over the hem at both ends of the strip of cotton, press and sew it in place.

FASTEN LEATHER PIECES to both ends of the crochet. Punch holes in the leather where you want to sew, then sew one piece folded double to the bottom end. Position the centre of the other piece in front of the small gap. Slip cotton cord through the folded top piece to act as a drawstring, then pass both ends underneath the upper leather strip and tie them to the lower leather loop. Cotton cord makes for a strong strap, or you can crochet a strap (see page 192).

THREE-YEAR-OLD MAYA stays cool while practising the game in her cute crocheted dress, adapted from the jumper on page 74.

BEE GAME

THE HIVE

SIZE

h: 16 cm (6¼ in)
d: from the middle 50 cm
(19¾ in)

YARN

Esteri hollow yarn, mustard
yellow 200 g (7 oz)

HOOK

7.0 mm
(K/10.5)

OTHER

Metal ring d: 10 cm (4 in),
leather strap l: 30 cm (12 in)

THE BEE

SIZE

l: 3 cm (1¼ in)
d: 7 cm (2¾ in)
wingspan: 3.5 cm (1⅜ in)

YARN

Eldorado, Puppets 10, black,
yellow, grey and off-white, a
small amount of each

HOOK

1.25 mm
(size 10)

OTHER

Oval wooden beads

**The summer's must-play challenge
has to be the bee game: how many
bees can you toss into the hive? If
there are two teams, crochet one
team's bees with yellow stripes and
the other's with grey. The team with
the most bees in the hive wins.**

THE HIVE

The hive is worked by crocheting double (single) crochet stitches in a tube, starting from the bottom. A metal ring is crocheted into the upper edge.

Rnd 1. Wrap yarn around your finger twice and crochet 9 dc (sc) into the loop. Crochet the yarn end together with a few of the stitches, and pull on it at the end of the round until there is no hole left.

Rnd 2. Move to the next round seamlessly in a spiral. Crochet 2 dc (sc) into each stitch.

Rnd 3. Crochet 2 dc (sc) into every other stitch, and 1 dc (sc) into each intervening stitch. The round consists of 27 dc (sc) in total.

Rnd 4. Crochet a dc(sc)-round without any increases.

Rnd 5. Crochet 2 dc (sc) into every third stitch, and 1 dc (sc) into each intervening stitch. The round consists of 36 dc (sc) in total.

Rnds 6–10. Crochet dc(sc)-rounds without any increases.

Rnd 11. Crochet 2 dc (sc) into every fourth stitch, and 1 dc (sc) into each intervening stitch. The round consists of 45 dc (sc) in total.

Rnds 12–15. Crochet dc(sc)-rounds without any increases.

Rnd 16. Decrease round. Crochet every fourth and fifth stitch together. To do this put the hook into the next stitch, yarn over hook and pull through. Repeat in the next stitch. There are now three stitches on your hook. Yoh and pull through all stitches on the hook. The first decrease is finished.

Rnd 17. Crochet a dc(sc)-round.

Rnd 18. Decrease round. In this round, crochet every third and fourth stitch together.

Rnd 19. Lay the metal ring on the edge, and crochet stitches by catching yoh from underneath the metal ring. Finish the edge with a round of ss. Cut the yarn and fasten off. Thread a leather strap through the crochet near the rim, punch holes and sew it into a loop.

THE BEE

Crochet grey stripes on half of the small bees and yellow on the other half to tell the two teams apart.

1 **Rnd 1.** Starting with the black yarn, make a slip knot on the hook and chain 2 stitches. Crochet 8 dc (sc) into the second chain stitch from the hook.
Rnd 2. Crochet 2 dc (sc) into each stitch.
Rnd 3. Crochet 2 dc (sc) into every second stitch, and crochet 1 dc (sc) into each intervening stitch. The round consists of 24 dc (sc) in total.
Rnds 4–6. Crochet a dc(sc)-round without increases.
Rnds 7–8. Change to the yellow yarn. Crochet dc(sc)-rounds.
Rnds 9–10. Change to the black yarn. Crochet dc(sc)-rounds.

2 Sew some eyes on the bee with off-white yarn.

3 **Rnds 11–12.** Change to the yellow yarn. Crochet dc(sc)-rounds.
Rnds 13–14. Change to the black yarn. Crochet dc(sc)-rounds. Slip a wooden bead inside the bee.

4 **Rnds 15–the end.** Decrease rounds. From rnd 15 onward, always crochet 2 dc (sc) together, until there are only a few stitches left in the round. Cut the yarn and fasten off.
The decrease-rounds shape a little stinger for the bee.

5

6

5 **Rnd 1.** Ch 9 stitches with off-white yarn for the wings. Work 6 treble (double) crochet stitches into the fourth stitch from the hook. Crochet 1 tr (dc) into the next four stitches, and another 7 tr (dc) into the last stitch. Crochet 1 tr (dc) into the next four stitches, and close the round with a slip stitch into the third chain stitch from the beginning.
Rnd 2. Ch 1, crochet 2 dc (sc) into the next five stitches. Crochet 1 dc (sc) into the next six stitches, and 2 dc (sc) into the fifth stitch of the wing edge. Crochet another 1 dc (sc) into five stitches and close the round with a ss into the beginning chain stitch. Cut the yarn and fasten off.

6 Sew the wings onto the bee with a few stitches. The bee is finished!

BASIC INSTRUCTIONS

5

HAND POSITION AND SLIP KNOT

1   Use the pencil grip when crocheting thin yarns to achieve a light touch.

2   Use the knife grip to crochet with rug cord and other thick yarns.

3   The first stitch on the hook is a slip knot. Take a yarn loop in between your thumb and index finger. Twist the free end around the loop and pull through the middle.

4   Put the hook through the larger loop. Tighten the loop around the hook. The slip knot is done.

5   Everyone has their preferred way of holding the yarn. In this three-finger hold, the yarn is held in the free hand with the fingers keeping the yarn taut.

6   While crocheting, the work is held in a tight grip between the thumb and the index finger.

CHAIN STITCH AND FINGER CROCHET

1 Make a slip knot on the hook. Wind the yarn over the hook, or twist the hook to go under the yarn, whichever you prefer.

2 Pull the yarn over hook through the loop.

3 Catch a new yarn over hook and pull through the stitch. Make sure that all chain stitches in the work are the same size and that your grip on the yarn stays tight enough.

4 You can also crochet chain stitches using your fingers, a technique best suited to thick and soft yarns.

5 Your fingers function as crochet hooks. Remember to keep your grip consistently tight so the stitches don't grow bigger.

6 A finger-crocheted surface is looser than one crocheted using a hook, but this technique can be useful for large projects, such as rugs.

DOUBLE (SINGLE) CROCHET BACK AND FORTH

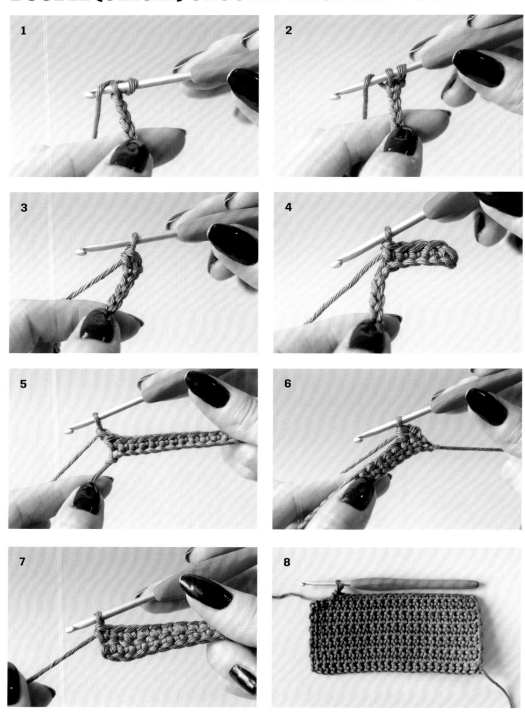

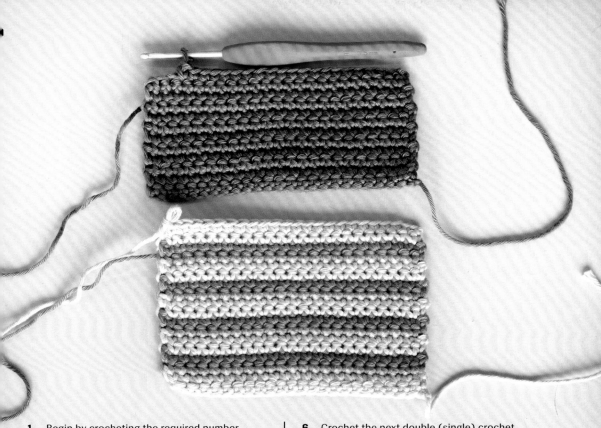

1. Begin by crocheting the required number of chain stitches. Put the hook through the second chain stitch from the hook. Catch the yarn over hook.

2. Pull the yarn through the stitch and catch the yarn over hook again.

3. Pull the yarn through both loops on the hook. You have made your first double (single) crochet stitch.

4. Continue crocheting one double (single) crochet stitch into every chain stitch.

5. At the end of the row, turn the work and chain one stitch to begin the next row. The chain stitch will count as the first double (single) crochet stitch of the row. Crochet the next double (single) crochet stitch into the second stitch from the hook, putting the hook through both loops of the stitch in the row below.

6. Crochet the next double (single) crochet stitch into the second stitch from the hook, putting the hook through both loops of the stitch in the row below.

7. Continue crocheting a double (single) crochet stitch into each stitch. Crochet the last double (single) crochet stitch into the beginning chain stitch.

8. Crochet the required number of rows. Remember to count your stitches now and again to make sure that the width of the work stays uniform. If the number of stitches changes, the work will either become wider or narrower.

9. You can crochet different types of patterns with double (single) crochet stitches. Experiment with the possibilities this technique offers.

DOUBLE (SINGLE) CROCHET IN A TUBE

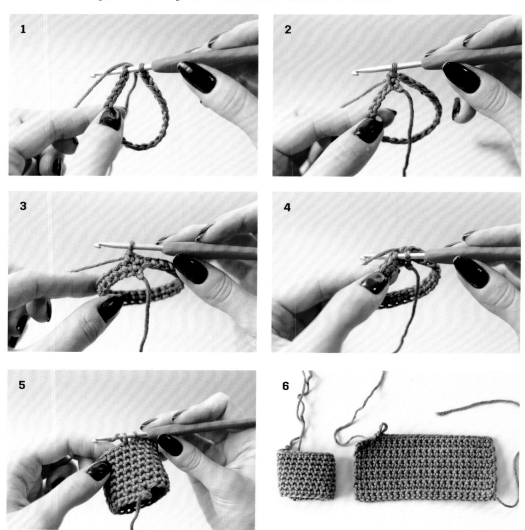

7

1. Begin by crocheting the required number of chain stitches. Make sure your chain isn't twisted, then put the hook through the first chain stitch.

2. Close into a ring by crocheting a double (single) crochet stitch.

3. Continue by crocheting one double (single) crochet stitch into each chain stitch.

4. Move seamlessly to the next round in a spiral. From now on, put the hook through both loops of the stitch in the row below.

5. A work crocheted in a tube won't show any seams at the rounds' start point, but the small loop steps will form.

6. The piece on the left of the photo is worked with double (single) crochet stitches in a tube, and the piece to the right is worked with double (single) crochet stitches back and forth. There is a significant difference in their surfaces. The surface crocheted in a tube is more even, whereas the surface worked back and forth shows both the right and wrong side of the double (single) crochet stitches.

7. You can crochet all kinds of tube-shaped items using this technique. While planning your patterns, note that the stitch will stack up in a staggered shape. Therefore, the pattern will turn a few degrees either to the left or the right. You can achieve a completely upright pattern by crocheting an optical double (single) crochet surface; by only putting the hook through the front loop of the stitch in the row below (see page 179).

TREBLE (DOUBLE) OR PILLARS BACK AND FORTH

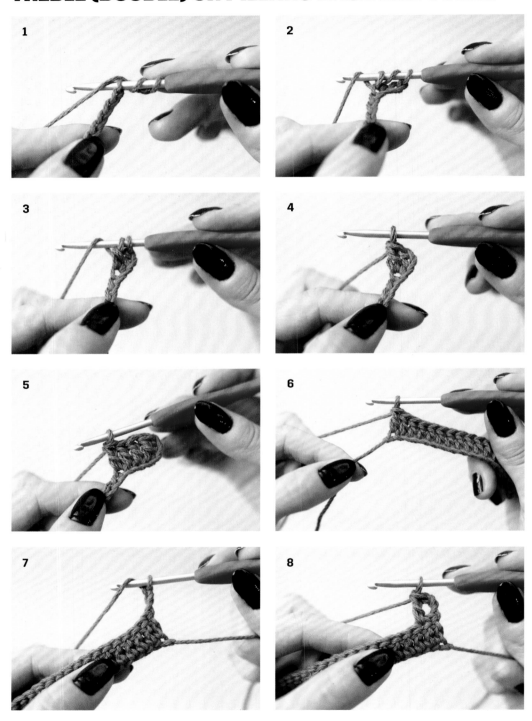

1   Crochet the required number of chain stitches. Catch the yarn over hook, put the hook through the fourth stitch from the hook, and catch the yarn over hook again.

2   Pull the yarn through the chain stitch, and catch the yarn over hook again.

3   Pull the yarn through two of the stitches on the hook, then catch the yarn over hook again.

4   Pull the yarn through the two remaining stitches on the hook. You have made one finished pillar. The three chain stitches at the edge count as the first pillar of the row.

5   Continue crocheting one pillar into each chain stitch.

6   Crochet the last pillar in the row into the first chain stitch.

7   On the second row, chain three stitches to begin. These form the first pillar in the row.

8   Crochet a pillar by putting the hook through both loops of the stitch in the row below.

9   Continue by crocheting a pillar into each pillar. Remember to count pillars now and again to make sure they are even across the rows.

TREBLE (DOUBLE) OR PILLARS IN A TUBE

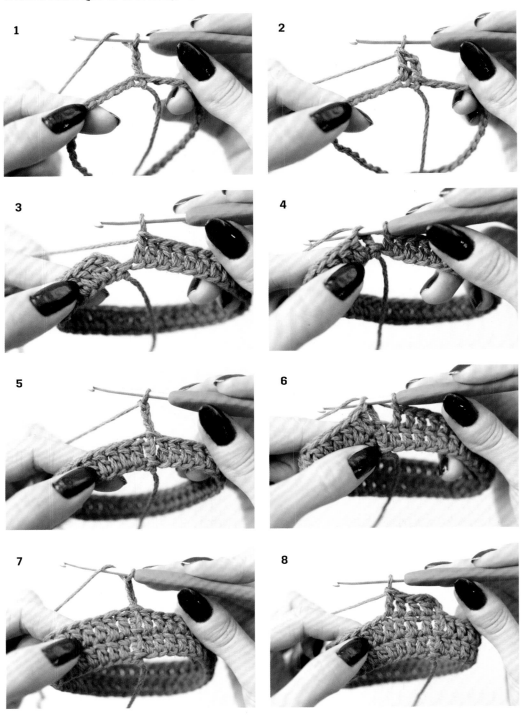

1 Start by crocheting the required number of chain stitches. Make sure your chain isn't twisted and close it into a ring with a slip stitch: put the hook through the first chain stitch, catch the yarn over hook and pull through to the right side of the work and through the stitch on your hook. Chain three stitches. These form the first pillar of the round.

2 Crochet one pillar into the next chain stitch.

3 Continue the round by crocheting one pillar into each chain stitch. Make sure you don't crochet another pillar at the start point; the last pillar is crocheted into the last chain stitch. A small gap at the start point might remain, but this will even out as your work grows.

4 Close the round by crocheting a slip stitch into the third chain stitch from the beginning.

5 On the next round, chain three stitches to begin. These form the first pillar of the round.

6 Crochet one pillar into each pillar, putting the hook through both loops of the stitch in the row below. Close the round with a slip stitch.

7 Always chain three stitches at the beginning of each new round.

8 Continue by crocheting one pillar into each pillar.

9 While crocheting pillars in a tube, the start point of the rounds will turn slightly to the right as the work grows. Because of this, the neckline seam on the wayfarer's jumper on page 74, for example, will show a little at the back of the jumper.

COLOUR CHANGE: DOUBLE (SINGLE) CROCHET

1

2

3

4

5

6

In a two-coloured double (single) crochet surface the non-working yarn is carried along within the stitches throughout.

1   At the colour-change point, put the hook through the stitch, and catch the yarn over hook. Carry the non-working yarn along by working it into the back of each stitch.

2   Pull the yarn over hook through the stitch.

3   Change yarns. Pull on the yarns a little to avoid loops forming on the wrong side of the work.

4   Catch the new colour yarn over hook.

5   Pull the yarn over hook through the stitch. The colour change is made by changing the colour of the stitch on the last yarn over hook of the stitch. This way the colour-change stays neat.

6   Continue crocheting using the new colour, and carry the non-working yarn along within the stitches throughout.

COLOUR CHANGE: TREBLE (DOUBLE) CROCHET

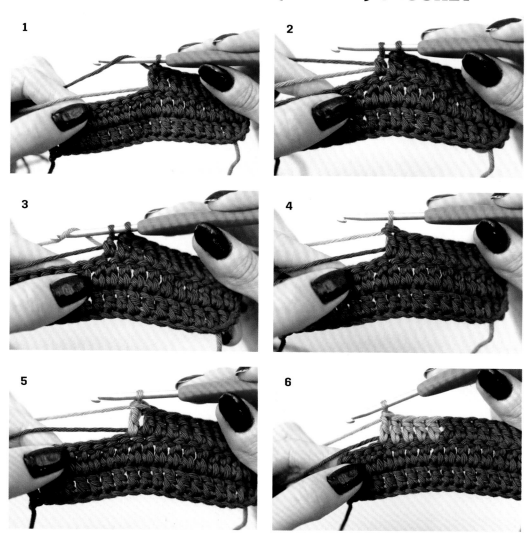

1

2

3

4

5

6

In a two-coloured pillar surface the non-working yarn is carried along within the stitches.

1 At the colour-change point, catch the yarn over hook. Carry the non-working yarn along by working it into the back of each stitch.

2 Crochet the next pillar to the last yarn over hook.

3 Change yarns. Pull a little on the yarn at this point to avoid loops forming on the wrong side of the work. Catch the new yarn over hook.

4 Pull the yarn over hook through both of the stitches on the hook. You have made one finished colour-change stitch.

5 Continue crocheting pillars with the new yarn, carrying the non-working yarn along within the pillars.

6 By changing the yarn colour on the last yarn over hook, the pattern's edge stays even.

SLIP STITCH

Slip stitch is used to strengthen an edge without increasing the size of the piece. It forms a strong edge on the right side of the work. Slip stitches are also used to close rounds.

1 Begin slip stitch as you would double (single) crochet. Put the hook through both loops of the stitch in the row below, and catch the yarn over hook.

2 Pull the yarn over hook through the crochet stitch.

3 Pull the stitch over hook through the stitch on the hook.

4 You have made one slip stitch.

5 Continue crocheting slip stitches for one round, then cut the yarn and fasten off.

SEWING SEAMS BY HAND

Seams in crochet work can be sewn closed using various stitches. They are usually sewn by hand, since using a machine can stretch the edge.

1   Sew the edges together one stitch at a time. Begin at one end and continue to the other end using short stitches. You can use different stitches, here backstitches are used.

2   Work back to the first end by sewing the stitches one more time. This way the seam becomes taut and even.

3   The photograph shows a hand-sewn seam. When sewing patterned crochet, take extra care to ensure that the patterns match on both sides of the seam.

TWO-COLOUR PILLAR SURFACE IN A TUBE

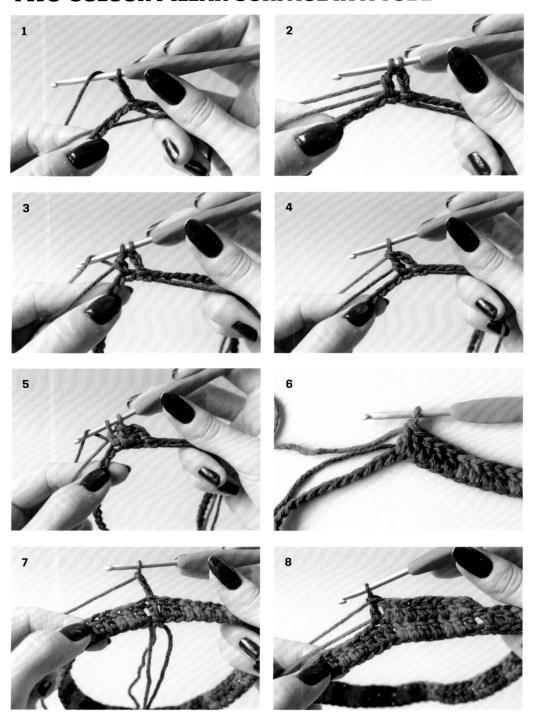

9

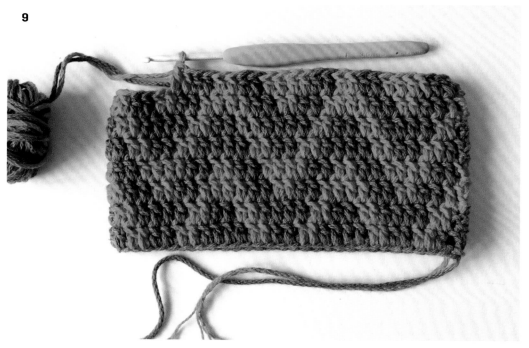

1 Begin by crocheting the required number of chain stitches with the first colour (blue). Check that your work isn't twisted. Join the round of chain stitches into a ring with a slip stitch: put the hook through the first chain stitch, catch the yarn over hook and pull through to the right side and through the stitch on the hook. Chain three stitches. These form the first pillar in the row. Catch the yarn over hook, and carry the second (red) yarn.

2 To change colour, crochet a pillar to the last yarn over hook, keeping the second yarn inside the lower edge of the pillar.

3 Catch the second yarn over hook, leaving the first yarn to carry along within the pillar.

4 Pull the yarn over hook through the stitches on the hook. You have made one finished colour-change stitch.

5 Crochet an entire pillar with this yarn; the colour will change at the last yarn over hook of the next pillar.

6 Continue crocheting pillars, one pillar into each chain stitch. Carry the non-working yarn along within the lower edges of the pillars. Change the yarn colours according to the pattern instructions.

7 Always chain three stitches to begin each row: these form the first pillar of each row.

8 Continue by crocheting one pillar into each pillar, putting the hook through both loops of the stitch in the row below. Carry the non-working yarn along at the second pillar. Change colours as needed.

9 The pattern will grow evenly while changing colours. You can crochet a variety of different patterns using this technique.

TWO-COLOUR PILLAR SURFACE BACK AND FORTH

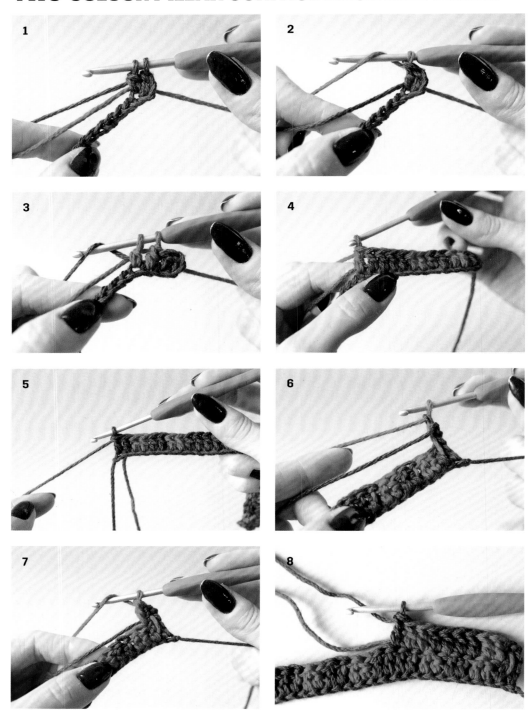

9

1 Begin by crocheting the required number of chain stitches with the first colour (blue). Put the hook through the fourth chain stitch from the hook, carry the second (red) yarn and crochet a pillar. The second yarn will remain within the lower edge of the pillar.

2 To change colour, crochet the next pillar to the last yarn over hook, then change to the second yarn to make the last yarn over hook. There is now a red stitch on the hook.

3 Crochet two pillars with the red yarn, while carrying the blue yarn along within the pillars. Change back to the blue yarn at the last yarn over hook of the next pillar.

4 Continue crocheting the row, changing colours following the chart. Carry the non-working yarn along within the pillars throughout, and always change the colour at the last yarn over hook of the pillars.

5 The last pillar in the row is crocheted without carrying the non-working yarn, which stays on the wrong side of the work.

6 Always chain three stitches at the beginning of each row: these form the first pillar in the row. The second pillar is crocheted with the red yarn in the pattern, so change colours at the third chain stitch.

7 Crochet a pillar with the red yarn. The blue yarn will be carried along within the pillars.

8 Continue crocheting, changing colours following the chart. Always drop the yarn being carried along one pillar from the end, and pick it back up at the second pillar after starting the next row. Always drop the yarn on the wrong side of the work.

9 Continue crocheting, following the chart.

RIBBED CROCHET

Ribbed crochet is used to make the wrist pieces for the fingerless mittens on page 82. You can also use it for warm scarves and socks.

1   Work the required number of chain stitches. Put the hook through the second chain stitch from the hook, and crochet one double (single) crochet stitch into each chain stitch. Chain one stitch at the beginning of the next row. This counts as the first double (single) crochet stitch of the next row.

2   Turn the work. Put the hook through only the back loop of the stitch in the previous row. Catch the yarn over hook and work double (single) crochet stitches.

3   Crochet double (single) crochet stitches to the end of this row, putting the hook through only the back loop of the stitch in the previous row.

4   Crochet the last stitch at the end of the row by putting the hook through both loops of the stitch in the previous row: this way you'll make the edge sturdier and more hardwearing. Always chain one stitch at the beginning of each row. Continue by crocheting double (single) crochet stitches, putting the hook through only the back loop of the stitch in the previous row.

FOR THE RIBBED CROCHET IN THE PHOTO I've used Lankava's soft Naturalia-wool. A neck warmer crocheted with this yarn will keep you toasty on the coldest of winter days.

PIXEL CROCHET

Pixel, or square, crochet is a versatile technique. You can plan patterns on squared paper and crochet items for different types of use.

1   Begin by crocheting the required number of chain stitches.

2   Catch the yarn over hook and put the hook through the seventh chain stitch from the hook. Catch the yarn over hook and pull the stitch through. Catch the yarn over hook again.

3   Pull the yarn over hook through two stitches on the hook. Catch the yarn over hook again, and pull through the two stitches on the hook. You have made one finished square.

4   Chain one stitch, miss (skip) one chain stitch and crochet a pillar. Your work now has two finished squares.

5   Continue by crocheting chain one, miss (skip) one and crochet a pillar. Repeat to the end

7 Crochet a pillar into the previous row's pillar.

8 To fill in a square with a pixel, crochet a pillar into the previous row's pillar, as well as a pillar in the chain stitch in between the previous row's pillars. Crochet yet another pillar into the next pillar on the previous row. One pixel is complete.

9 Continue crocheting squares and pixels, following the chart.

10 Be careful to always crochet the pixels in the right places.

11 You can crochet all kinds of patterns and motifs using pixel crochet, and you can use any type of yarn.

of the row. If your chain has too many stitches, open the slip knot and unravel the surplus chain stitches. Your work won't unravel further because chain stitches lock into place while crocheting. Leave one stitch for finishing. If your work contains too few stitches, you can continue chaining stitches using the yarn end.

6 Always chain four stitches when starting a new row.

YARNS USED
IN THIS BOOK

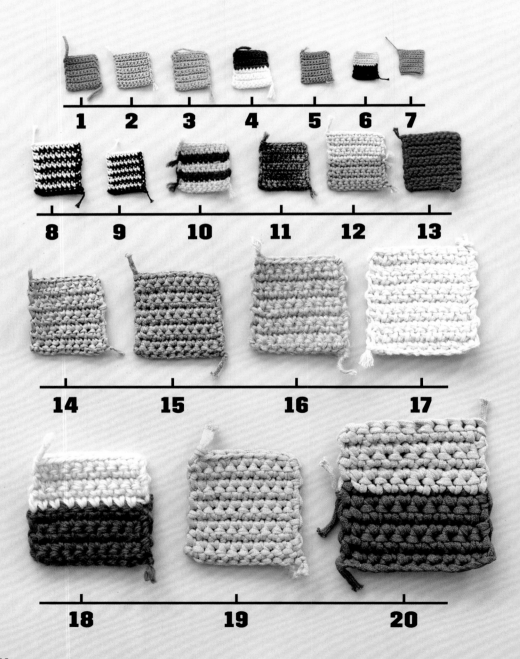

NO.	NAME OF YARN	MATERIAL	AMOUNT	THE MAKE	YARN SOLD BY
1	Millamia, Naturally Soft Merino	100% merino wool	Ball 50 g (1¾ oz)/ approx. 125 m	Neck warmer	Lentävä Lapanen
2	Hilos, La Espiga	100% nylon	Roll 200 g (7 oz)	Bike bag	Laavikko
3	Sirdar, Cotton DK	100% cotton	Ball 100 g (3½ oz)/ approx. 212 m	Travel mirror	Laavikko, Snurre
4	Schachenmayr, Merino Extrafine 120	100% merino wool	Ball 50 g (1¾ oz)/ approx. 120 m	Carry cushion	Lentävä Lapanen
5	Schachenmayr, Catania Fine	100% cotton	Ball 50 g (1¾ oz)/ approx. 165 m	Yarn chain	Coats Opi
6	Eldorado Puppets 10	100% cotton	Ball 50 g (1¾ oz)/ approx. 265 m	Bee game: bee	Lankasatama
7	Maharaja Silk Yarn	100% silk	Skein 50 g (1¾ oz)/ approx. 300 g (10½ oz)	Bow tie	Vihreä Vyyhti
8	Liina fish net twine, 18-ply	100% cotton	Roll 500 g (1 lb 2 oz)/ approx. 840 m	Folk bag, Football bag, Bunting	Suomen Lanka, Lankava
9	Liina fish net twine, 12-ply	100% cotton	Roll 500 g (1 lb 2 oz)/ approx. 1280 m	Poster, Band poster, Toiletry bag, Mat bag, Anchor pocket	Suomen Lanka, Lankava
10	Gepard, Sømands Garn	100% wool	Skein 150 g (5 oz)/approx. 280 m	Wayfarer's jumper	Snurre
11	Madelinetosh, Sock	100% merino wool	Skein 100g (3½ oz)/ approx. 360 m	Fingerless mittens	Snurre, TitiTyy
12	Schachenmayr, Catania Grande	100% cotton	Ball 50 g (1¾ oz)/ approx. 63 m	Passport bag, Lumberjack's backpack	Coats Opti
13	Lamana, Ica	100% cotton	Ball 50 g (1¾ oz)/ approx. 80 m	Speaker slipcase, Anchor bag, Can carrier	Snurre
14	Adriafil, Rafia	100% frond thread	Skein 25 g (1 oz)	Bowler hat	Snurre
15	Putkis hollow yarn	100% cotton	Skein approx. 500 g (1 lb 2 oz)	Slippers, men's and women's	Toika
16	Jute yarn	100% jute	Cone 1 kg (2 lb 3 oz)/ 450 m	Storage basket	Lankava
17	Moppari spiral yarn	75% recycled cotton, 25% acrylic	Roll 1 kg (2 lb 3 oz)/ approx. 310 m	Log carrier	Suomen Lanka, Lankava
18	Muhku wool yarn	100% wool	Cone 1 kg (2 lb 3 oz)/ approx. 390 m	Chequered rug	Lankava
19	Esteri hollow yarn	100% polyester	Roll 1 kg (2 lb 3 oz)/ approx. 330 m	Bee game: hive	Lankava
20	Lilli hollow yarn	80% recycled cotton, 20% other fibres	Skein 1 kg (2 lb 3 oz)/ approx. 220 m	Pattern rug	Lankava

MAINTENANCE

6

WHITTLING A CROCHET HOOK

Crochet hooks are made out of many different materials, with bamboo, wood, plastic, aluminium and steel being the more common materials. You can find old wooden crochet hooks at antiques markets, but you can also whittle one yourself. Here, my father and I are searching for suitable whittling materials in the forests of northern Karelia. Durable and flexible types of wood, such as junipers, maples or birches, are particularly appropriate for crochet hooks. We found a good juniper, and broke off the bottom two branches.

You'll need a good knife for whittling. The blade doesn't need to be long, but the handle must be sturdy. For the hook you will need a knotless piece of wood about 20 cm (8 in) long. We have made two hooks here, the equivalent to an 8.0 mm and a 12.0 mm – referring to the diameter of the head. Carving a smaller hook is pointless, since it will quickly snap, but you can carve gigantic hooks, or a collection of beautiful hooks whittled from different kinds of wood.

1   Working on an area of about 10 cm (4 in) at one end of the juniper branch, start peeling in the direction of growth, stripping the branch of its outer layers. You can leave the bark on the handle piece untouched and just peel the hook end, as shown here. Leave the peeled wood to dry for a few days, since wood that is whittled while wet may later split as it dries.

2   Draw the shape of the hook onto the peeled end of the branch. Leave a thickness of about half the handle at the neck of the hook. Here, a small hole has been drilled into the deepest part of the hook end to make it easier to work. Using a thin-blade jigsaw, saw the profile of the hook by following the drawn lines.

3 Begin whittling the hook shape. Carefully whittle the round shape of the head using light strokes and always aiming away from yourself. Patience and precision are important while doing this. In the photo above, my father is whittling the neck of the hook; the end is already sawed and whittled into a round shape. The head of the hook has to be deep enough that even thick stitches will stay on the hook while crocheting.

4 Sand the neck and deepest part of the head using light strokes. You can leave the head coarsely shaped, as here.

THE FINISHED HOOK is 12 mm in size, and its head is whittled into an angular shape. The neck of the hook has to be wear-resistant, so give it a light flexibility test. If the hook breaks and turns into sauna-kindling, make sure the neck of your next hook is thicker.

Crochet-hook handles are often flattened in the middle to make them more ergonomic in use. When making your own crochet hooks, you can peel the whole branch and shape the hook to your hand. You could also choose a naturally curving branch for your hook.

261

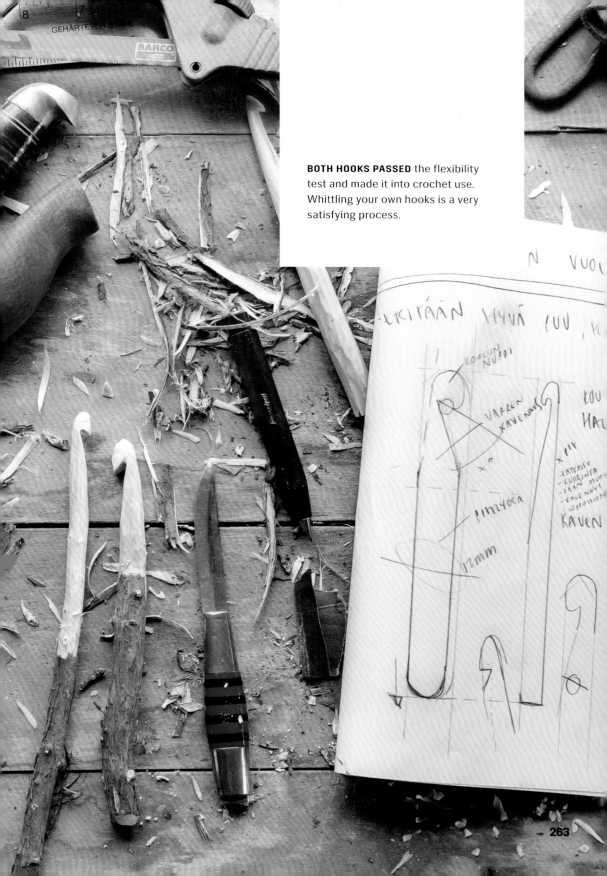

BOTH HOOKS PASSED the flexibility test and made it into crochet use. Whittling your own hooks is a very satisfying process.

CROCHETER'S STRETCHING

Crafting for periods of time can leave you with stiff limbs and achy muscles. These exercises my brother, Pasi, a yoga instructor, is demonstrating will help you to loosen up. Perform the stretches calmly and while listening to your body. When a stretch feels right, stay in that position. Breathe in through your nose and out again slowly, allowing the stretch to deepen along with your breathing.

1   Sit cross-legged, straight-backed, shoulders relaxed and with your hands resting in your lap. Gently stretch your neck by slowly tilting your head to the sides and carefully back and forth.

 1-3 min

1-3 min

2 Sit cross-legged. On the in-breath, spread your arms out to the sides and open up your chest. On the out-breath, bring your arms together in front of you, with straight arms throughout.

1-3 min/each side

3 Stretch one leg out in front of you and carefully reach the same hand towards your toes. Keeping your back straight, lightly push your hips forward, lean towards your toes and stretch your side. Stretch to the other side as well.

🕐 **1-3 min**

4 Lift your hips, keeping your back and legs straight and pushing your chin towards your chest. Breathe calmly and deeply through your nose and relax your body.

🕐 **3-5 min**

5 Stretch your arms in front of you and relax your shoulders and back. Carefully push your backside towards your heels.

Finally, assume a relaxed cross-legged position. Sit at ease on the ground with hands resting in your lap, legs relaxed and back straight. Focus on taking deep breaths and let your body slowly relax.

TIP! Wrap up warm for al-fresco stretching with a tube scarf made from merino wool.

Use a tree trunk if outside, or a wall when inside, to help you stretch
your back, shoulders and sides. Stay in each position for about a minute.
Breathe calmly and enjoy!

OTHER MATERIALS USED IN THIS BOOK

YARNS

p. 32 **BOWLER HAT** Katia Love Wool. Lentävä Lapanen

p. 83 **FINGERLESS MITTENS** Madelinetosh. Sport, TitiTyy ja Snurre

p. 106 **CHILDREN'S SLIPPERS** Cascade. Heathers, Snurre

p. 114 **KNALLI** Fibra Natura, Raffia. Lankava

p. 114 **CHAIN BRACELET** DMC Petra 5. Eiran Langat

p. 129 **STRIPED WALLET** Schachenmayr, Catania. Coats Opi

p. 224 **MAYA'S DRESS** Lang, Gamma. Eiran Langat

p. 258 **RED WOOL JUMPER** (a variant of the jumper) Debbie Bliss. Paloma. Snurre and Kerä.

p. 269 **BRICK PATTERNED SCARF** (a variant of the toiletry bag) BC Yarn, Semilla Grosso. Snurre.

OTHER

p. 13 **ERGONOMIC HOOKS** Clover and Coats Opti

p. 17 **CUSHION INSERTS** Lennol

p. 35 **NYLON REINFORCEMENT** Paapo

p. 40 **PLASTIC TUBE** Lankava

p. 105 **WOOL INSOLES** Rintalan Tila

p. 108 **WOVEN PIXEL RUG** Molla Mills for Forme

p. 206 **FABRIC SPRAY** Taika-lehti

p. 208 **MEN'S COSMETIC PRODUCTS** Frantsilan luomuyrttitila

p. 219 **MAT BAG'S STRAPS** Katia, Cotton cord. Lentävä Lapanen

FABRICS, LEATHER Eurokangas
BUTTONS, ZIPS, LEATHER POCKETS Nappitalo
METAL PIECES, RIMS Sinelli
LEATHER BELTS Varusteleka

IN COOPERATION WITH

A special thanks to Lankava

Clover
Coats Opi
Colorblind Patterns
Eiran Langat
Eurokangas
Forme
Käpynen
Lankakauppa TitiTyy
Lankasatama
Lavikko
Lentävä Lapanen
Nappitalo
O.P.I
Paapo
Rintalan Tila
Sinelli
Snurre
Suomen Lanka
Taika-lehti
Toika
Varusteleka
Vihreä Vyyhti
Wollen Berlin

PHOTOGRAPH LOCATIONS

Good Life Coffee
Studio Linnunlaulu
Huvikumpu, Nurmes
Käpylän Lippakioski
Kolin kansallispuisto
Nosturi
Siltanen
Ravintola Lie Mi

THANKS

Annastiina, Noak, Aarni, Hilla and Pasi Leppälä
Anu Turu, Taika Lehti
Daniel Arab, Colorblind Patterns
Elina Järvinen, Praktik
Eiji Satsuki and Jaana Leppälä
Emili and Maya Satsuki
Jaakko Ruotsalainen
Jani Pensola, Custom Wood
Jarno Lukkarila, Typolar
Jonne Järvelä, Korpiklaani
Kai Kuusisto
Kirsti and Jyri Karppinen, Lankava
Laura Pehkonen and Miikka Pirinen
The Linkola family
Mickael Gerwig
Minna Leppälä
Niko Hyttinen, One Morning Left
Niko Mikkonen
Paul Takahashi
Ruta Sluskaite, Wollen Berlin
Saara ja Marco, Atelieri O. Haapala
Samu Sundell
Toomas Laine
Topi Vihermalmi
Tuppu Ritola, Tatuata
Unto Helo, Rytmihäiriö

Big brother and father